Sexual Health and Black College Students

This book explores the various psychosocial, sociocultural, and contextual factors that affect the sexual health of Black students who attend Historically Black Colleges and Universities (HBCUs), and how this environment can help develop strategies to improve sexual health outcomes for its students.

The college environment provides young people with a new sense of independence, self-determination, and peer pressure to engage in risky sexual behaviors, and research has shown that Black students at HBCUs bear a disproportionate burden of poorer sexual health outcomes than students at predominately white institutions (PWIs). Uniquely focusing on the sexual milieu of Black students, Hall-Byers explains why a better understanding of these settings is needed to guide successful interventions that benefit and support the sexual health of Black students. Chapters compare data and research on sexual health outcomes of young Black men and women in comparison to those at PWIs, as well as looking at the role of HBCU campus contexts and cultures, the potential psychosocial and sociocultural influences, what culturally responsive approaches may look like, and recommendations on how HBCU campuses can increase positive sexual health, such as through access, collaborative efforts among administrative offices, and reallocating resources.

Sexual Health and Black College Students aims to advance the translation of culturally grounded research into effective practice and is essential reading for researchers and practitioners in sex therapy, public health, and social science as well as for college health staff, including nurses, student affairs, and campus wellness centers.

Dr. Naomi M. Hall-Byers is a professor of psychology in the Department of Psychological Sciences at Winston-Salem State University (WSSU). She is the Director of the Race, Culture, and Context (RC^2) lab and her overarching program of research focuses on psychological, social, cultural, and contextual factors associated with health disparities and inequities among youth and emerging adults (YEAs) of African descent.

Leading Conversations on Black Sexualities and Identities

Series editor: James C. Wadley

Leading Conversations on Black Sexualities and Identities aims to stimulate sensitive conversations and teachings surrounding Black sexuality. Written by academics and practitioners who have dedicated their work to the distinctive sexual and relational experiences of persons of African descent, the series aims to provoke an enhanced understanding throughout the field of sexology and identify educational and clinical strategies for change. Amplifying issues and voices often minimalized and marginalized, this series is a continuation and expansion of inquiry and advocacy upon the complexities and nuances of relational negotiation, identity affirmation, critical discourse, and liberated sexual expression.

Titles in the series:

"Finally! The field of Black sexuality studies has a comprehensive narrative of the experiences of Black young adults who attend HBCUs. Hall-Byers meticulously constructs a research, clinical, and educational portrait that captures the complex behavioral and affective nuances that impacts sexual decision making of Black students. Indeed, this is a must read for all sexuality educators at HBCUs and PWIs."

James C. Wadley, Ph.D., *Lincoln University, USA*

"This book provides a better understanding of the sexual health needs of Black college students at HBCUs. The book explores the intersectionality of sex, race, and culture on public health outcomes for a marginalized, yet revered sub-population. This important context is critical to inform decisions about sex and relationships, and key for mitigating contextual factors in an effort to advance sexual health for Black students!"

Thomas Alex Washington, Ph.D., *professor and co-director, Center for Health Equity Research Institute, College of Health & Human Services, California State University, Long Beach, USA*

"This is a timely book that contextualizes the sexual health of Black college students, specifically at HBCUs. The integration of theory, research, applications, and practice by Dr. Hall-Byers draws readers attention and provides critical strategies to improve the sexual health of our students. I look forward to using this book in my courses!"

Danielle Dickens, Ph.D., *Spelman College, USA*

"This book is much needed and fills a very important gap that has long existed regarding the sexual health of Black College Students at the Intersections of their social identities, lived experiences, and the social environment. Hall-Byers successfully provides educators, researchers, administrators, and health professionals with valuable insights and knowledge that can assist their health education and health promotion activities when planning and delivering interventions for Black College Students at HBCU's. Grounded in a sex positive lens, this textbook also provides important factors to consider when addressing sexual health and the use of social justice informed approaches in order to prevent stigmatization and marginalization due to social identity."

Yarneccia D. Dyson, PhD., *University of North Carolina Greensboro, USA*

Sexual Health and Black College Students

Exploring the Sexual Milieu
of HBCUs

Naomi M. Hall

Routledge
Taylor & Francis Group

NEW YORK AND LONDON

First published 2022
by Routledge
605 Third Avenue, New York, NY 10158

and by Routledge
4 Park Square, Milton Park, Abingdon, Oxon, OX14 4RN

*Routledge is an imprint of the Taylor & Francis Group, an
informa business*

© 2022 Naomi M. Hall

Library of Congress Cataloguing-in-Publication Data
Names: Hall, Naomi M., author.
Title: Sexual health and Black college students : exploring the
sexual milieu of HBCUs / Naomi M. Hall.
Description: New York, NY : Routledge, 2023. | Includes
bibliographical references and index. |
Identifiers: LCCN 2022010372 (print) | LCCN 2022010373
(ebook) | ISBN 9781032325668 (paperback) | ISBN
9781032015705 (hardback) | ISBN 9781003180944 (ebook)
Subjects: LCSH: College students, Black--Sexual behavior. |
College students, Black--Psychology. | African American
universities and colleges.
Classification: LCC HQ35.2 .H35 2023 (print) | LCC HQ35.2
(ebook) | DDC 306.70835--dc23/eng/20220304
LC record available at https://lccn.loc.gov/2022010372
LC ebook record available at https://lccn.loc.gov/2022010373

ISBN: 978-1-032-01570-5 (hbk)
ISBN: 978-1-032-32566-8 (pbk)
ISBN: 978-1-003-18094-4 (ebk)

DOI: 10.4324/9781003180944

Typeset in Times New Roman
by MPS Limited, Dehradun

I want to thank my husband (Kevin) and my daughter (Saige) for supporting me while I pursue my many interests and passions, and for giving me the space to do them. Many thanks to my family members, those related by blood or chosen by love, who are always encouraging, honest, and supportive. I am appreciative to the many faculty, staff, and students who know the value and power of HBCUs and work tirelessly to ensure that tomorrow shines just a little brighter than it did today for our students. HBCU love is different! Finally, my greatest acknowledgment is for my two favorite ancestors (Jessie and Catherine Hall) who provided guidance, wisdom, and an enduring legacy of love and laughter.

Contents

Foreword

When I met Dr. Hall Byers at a conference several years ago, we had a wonderful conversation about working at our own respective HBCU's. At the time, she maintained a tenure track position at Winston Salem State University while I was faculty at Lincoln University (Pennsylvania). We spent some time talking about how HBCUs had evolved over the past 15–20 years in their effort to address sexuality-related issues. I shared that my university was in an active discussion about how gender roles are constructed and how centuries worth of patriarchal conversations were negatively impacting policy and programs. She shared that her institution was in the midst of having dialogue about HIV/AIDS prevention campaigns to reduce the likelihood of acquiring sexually transmitted infections. At both institutions, there needed to be a conceptual shift from faculty, staff, and students *not talking about sensitive issues* to formally and informally engaging in meaningful conversations that can transform and empower folks to be their best selves and have healthy relationships. While our individual universities had begun to develop programming that specifically targeted sexual health and wellness, there was much work (e.g., research, programming, policy changes, etc.) to be done that would consider race while addressing homophobic, transphobic, sexist, and patriarchal rhetoric and how these constructs impact sexuality expression as well as the maintenance of identities (individual and collective).

Over the years, Dr. Hall Byers and I continued our discussion about the two of us evolving in the academy and the impact we could possibly have in administrative, faculty, and clinical roles. We acknowledged the scarcity of tenure track Black faculty who focus on sexuality. Even though there are a greater number of Black faculty at HBCUs than at predominantly White institutions (PWIs), some in professoriate shy away from developing sexuality research agendas.

This seems problematic as our country continues to be challenged by skewed ideologies and behaviors regarding sexual assault (e.g., R. Kelly, Bill Cosby); exploring the idea and experiences of gender non-binary folks; the use of social media as a means of relational and sexual partner selection; and understanding the utility of sex positivity programming. Thus, it seems necessary for HBCUs to consider creating tenure track positions that invite Black sexuality scholars to teach, mentor, and maintain a research agenda that addresses the sexual health needs of persons of African descent. Moreover, consideration should be given to developing more Black clinical practitioners to become sexuality therapists and consultants. Doing so may allow for an enhanced number of professionals who could assist the university and its constituents in unpacking and unraveling relational and sexual health issues.

Dr. Hall Byers continues to lead the discussion about sexuality and sexual health and has proven to be a thought leader in field of race and sexuality studies. In the present initiative, she offers us her research and insight entitled, *Sexual Health & Black College Students: Exploring the Sexual Milieu of Historically Black Colleges and Universities.* She invites scholars and practitioners to think critically about how HBCU's have been able to meet the academic and sexual wellness needs of its students over time, context, and circumstance. She eloquently acknowledges that even though some HBCU's are challenged by a lack of resources, they remain at the forefront for producing young, Black leaders who actively engage in discussions about sexual wellness. In addition, Dr. Hall Byers meticulously dives into the world of courtship, sexual decision making, and the continuum of Black sexual expression of college students. Because of this contribution to the literature and field of sexuality studies, scholars and practitioners are in a more advantageous position to follow Dr. Hall Byers lead in creating conversations about Black sexualities and identities at HBCUs.

James C. Wadley, Series Editor

1 Introduction

The purpose of this book is to explore various psychosocial, socio-cultural, and contextual factors critical to the sexual health of Black college students within the milieu of Historically Black Colleges and Universities (HBCUs). Additionally, it explores how this environment can promote, or in some cases impede, optimal sexual health. The book can be used to help guide the development of strategies and interventions to improve sexual health outcomes and advance the translation of culturally grounded research into effective practice. This chapter is introductory in that it explores the definition of sexual health, its importance, and the history and significance of HBCUs in the United States.

The World Health Organization (WHO) and the Centers for Disease Control and Prevention (Centers for Disease Control and Prevention, 2019) define sexual health as a state of physical, emotional, mental, and social well-being in relation to sexuality. Although the terms are often used interchangeably, sexual health is more than sexuality or sexual behaviors (Younge et al., 2014). It is multi-dimensional and includes the ability to comprehend the benefits, risks, and responsibilities of sexual experiences while also understanding the importance of preventing disease and other adverse outcomes. Additionally, it includes access to comprehensive, *accurate* sex and sexuality-related information and services, and to be in an environment that affirms and promotes sexual health (World Health Organization, 2015). Often only the negative consequences for individuals are discussed in the literature and the media such as sexually transmitted infection (STI) and Human immunodeficiency virus (HIV) rates, unplanned pregnancies, and sexual violence. However, numerous other areas of sexual health should receive more attention because they are important to one's overall well-being. Areas such as identity (e.g., racial/ethnic, gender, sexual), decision-making, sexual expression, relationships, and sexual pleasure are often

DOI: 10.4324/9781003180944-1

neglected for a discussion about physiological and/or physical disease. Sexual health is a critical part of a person's overall health and development (Hogben et al., 2017), and unfortunately, there is a dearth of empirical studies examining this topic, particularly among young Black college students.

The Surgeon General's *Call to Action to Promote Sexual Health and Responsible Sexual Behavior* (2001) was the first formal recognition of the need to comprehensively promote sexuality, sexual health, and responsible sexual behavior to enhance population health by the United States (US) government. Decades of work in public health and health promotion indicate that knowledge alone is insufficient for sustained and/or changed behavior. Sexual health is not merely the absence of disease, it encompasses so much more (e.g., identity, expression, pleasure) and has a lifelong impact on your overall health and well-being, identity, and relationships. As one moves through the various topics and chapters, keep in mind that it is the complex relationship between one's affect, behavior, and cognition (ABCs) that dictates whether one enacts protective, or risky, practices throughout the lifespan. A brief explanation follows:

- *Affect*, or an emotional component to sexual health is akin to one's attitude about something. Thurstone (1931) notes that an attitude is the *"affect for or against a psychological object"* (p. 261) and is inherently a subjective aggregate of feelings toward something. Emotions attached to a thought or action related to sexual health are integral in the manifestation of outcomes. While this book is not focused on methodological approaches, it is safe to say there are numerous ways to measure affect or attitudes toward something, but none are without limitations. One of the major challenges of researching affect and/or attitudes is that they are not functioning outside of the social environment in which the individual lives and operates. There are some aspects of sexual health that may solely be based on an individual's decision to engage in a behavior, but in sexual health, affect and attitude toward a behavior may be deeply rooted in the emotions attached to a partner or partners.
- *Behavior* is an observable action by an individual or group. Either a person uses a condom, or they do not. Either a person regularly schedules, and attends, preventive health assessments (e.g., pap smears, prostate exams) or they do not. To observe a behavioral outcome is simple; however, to understand what occurred prior to that outcome is much more complex and requires an understanding of factors (i.e., affect and cognition) associated with the decision-making process.

- *Cognition* is the mental process involved in knowledge acquisition, acknowledgment, and comprehension. Some may believe that having knowledge about a topic is sufficient for making the 'right' decision. However, it is known from research and life experience that knowledge of something does not necessarily translate to a particular behavior. For example, most Millennials (born between 1981 and 1995) and Generation Z (born between 1996 and 2010) college students received some variation of sexuality education in middle and/or high school. Except for abstinence-only education, young people are taught about contraception and using condoms to prevent pregnancy and STIs, including HIV. While the teenage pregnancy rates have steadily declined since the 1990s, the rates of STI infection and transmission have not. This should prompt questions about certain decisions and behaviors that are under the direct volition of an individual, such as taking birth control pills. However, when one or more other individuals are involved, a negotiation occurs. This negotiation can be directly, or indirectly communicated between parties involved. Either way, the intersection of personal and social environment is fundamental to how sexual health is enacted.

The importance of examining sexual health among all citizens is important, and specifically focusing on young Black college students cannot be overstated. During a focus group with the author, a 19-year-old HBCU student said, *"College is a great time to really get in touch with your sexual self. However, you hardly ever get anyone talking to you about it."* It is as valuable as any other type of health, yet it is neglected because there may be negative emotions such as shame, fear, confusion, embarrassment, and anger associated with it. Sexual health outcomes for young Black college students remain disproportionately worse than college students of other racial/ethnic groups (Buhi et al., 2010; Younge et al., 2018). The southern states account disproportionally for these poor sexual health outcomes among Black college students (Centers for Disease Control and Prevention, 2019; Younge et al., 2013), and especially those attending Historically Black Colleges and Universities (HBCUs) are at increased risk for poorer sexual health outcomes.

There are several psychosocial and sociocultural factors that influence how young Black college students define and experience their sexual health. While no resource is all-encompassing, each section of this book makes a concerted effort to focus on information from a wide variety of sources to provide an overview of the sexual milieu of Black college students attending HBCUs. The author hopes that this information will be utilized in the design and implementation of studies, programs, and policies that take a culturally responsive approach to focusing on the sexual health of young Black college students, particularly those attending HBCUs. Throughout this book the terms 'culturally relevant' and 'culturally responsive' will be used repeatedly as the author believes that these approaches are critical to addressing, reducing, and eliminating the sexual health disparities that exist in this population. When the term *culturally relevant* is used, it is meant to refer to the use of cultural references to deliver material in hopes of imparting knowledge, skills, and attitudes to a population or subpopulation (Ladson-Billings, 1995). However, *culturally responsive* is meant to imply an approach that emphasizes learning from and relating respectfully with individuals in your own culture and those from other cultures. It is important to acknowledge that culture is more than a substitute for race and/or ethnicity, it is a life-affirming code of conduct. The next section gives an overview of HBCUs, their relevance in the lives of Black students, and how the culture and environment is unlike any other type of educational institution experience.

The Significance of Historically Black Colleges and Universities

The Higher Education Act of 1965 defines an HBCU as *"any historically Black college or university that was established before 1964, whose principal mission was, and is, the education of Black Americans, and that is accredited by a nationally recognized accrediting agency or association determined by the Secretary [of Education] to be a reliable authority as to the quality of training offered or is, according to such an agency or association, making reasonable progress toward accreditation."* HBCUs were established to educate formerly enslaved people, and most were established shortly after the American Civil War (1861–1865) through the year 1964. Before the American Civil War, there were no institutions of higher education for Black students. Although three institutions were created before 1861: 1) Cheyney University of Pennsylvania (1837); 2) Lincoln University (1854); and 3) Wilberforce University (1856), they were originally designed to provide elementary and secondary schooling for students without previous education (United States Department of Education [US DoE], 1991). The majority of HBCUs were established between 1865 and 1900, with 1867 being the year with the greatest number of HBCUs founded. The Morrill Act of 1862 is a United States statute that allowed for the creation of land-grant colleges using the profits from sales of federal land obtained

Table 1.1 List of HBCU Land-Grant Institutions

State	Institution	Year of Establishment
Alabama	Alabama A&M University	1875
Alabama	Tuskegee University	1881
Arkansas	The University of Arkansas at Pine Bluff	1873
Delaware	Delaware State University	1891
Florida	Florida A&M University	1887
Kentucky	Kentucky State University	1886
Louisiana	Southern University	1880
Maryland	University of Maryland Eastern Shore	1886
Missouri	Lincoln University	1866
Mississippi	Alcorn State University	1871
North Carolina	North Carolina A&T State University	1891
Ohio	Central State University	1887
Oklahoma	Langston University	1897
Pennsylvania	Fort Valley State University	1895
South Carolina	South Carolina State University	1896
Tennessee	Tennessee State University	1912
Texas	Prairie View A&M University	1876
Virgin Islands	University of the Virgin Islands	1962
Virginia	Virginia State University	1882
Washington, D.C.	University of the District of Columbia	1851
West Virginia	West Virginia State University	1891

from indigenous tribes. The Second Morrill Act of 1890 established a separate land-grant institution for Black students in states where land-grant institutions for White students were established (*see* Table 1.1). Today, there are 21 land-grant institutions established to serve Black students (Association of Public & Land-grant Universities, n.d.).

There are also predominately Black institutions (PBIs) which were founded after 1964 and, according to the Higher Education Act of 2008, must meet the following criteria: 1) enroll at least 40% African American students; 2) have a minimum of 1,000 undergraduates; 3) have at least 50% low-income or first-generation degree-seeking undergraduate students; and 4) have a low per full-time undergraduate student expenditure in comparison with other institutions offering similar instruction (Thurgood Marshall College Fund [TMCF], 2019). Together, HBCUs and PBIs, provide access to higher education and continue to contribute substantially to the upward mobility of Black students and students of all races and ethnicities.

Student Population

While HBCUs represent only 3% of colleges/universities, the enrollment of Black college students (undergraduate and graduate) is approximately 10% nationwide, and they award 17% of bachelor's degrees to Black students (National Center for Educational Statistics [NCES], 2016). Degree conferment increases to 24% for Black undergraduates in science, technology, engineering, and mathematics (STEM) majors. The rates of enrollment and degree conferment are illuminated when looking at states where HBCUs are located, such as North Carolina. HBCUs make up 16% of the four-year institutions in North Carolina (n = 9) but enroll 45% of all Black undergraduate students and award 43% of all bachelor's degrees to Black students in the state (Saunders & Nagle, 2018). The UNCF publication, *HBCUs Punching Above Their Weight*, notes that despite being institutions that traditionally have not had sufficient financial resources, the impact that HBCUs have on students, the surrounding communities, and their local and regional economies is significant.

> *"When sports writers say that boxers punch above their weight, they mean that they hit harder than would be predicted from their weight alone. So, when UNCF says that HBCUs punch above their weight, we mean that, given their small average size, and given that they have been historically under-resourced, the impact of these unique institutions is significantly greater than one would expect."*
>
> (Saunders & Nagle, 2018, p.3)

The hashtag *#HBCUStrong* was introduced on social media platforms and sparked an outpouring of alumni, faculty, staff, students, and family and community members giving their accounts of the HBCU experience.

In 2018, there were 101 accredited HBCUs in 19 states, the District of Columbia, and the United States (US) Virgin Islands. Of these, 51 are public institutions, 50 are private institutions, and combined they enrolled approximately 300,000 students in 2018 (NCES, 2020). Private HBCUs tend to be smaller, more costly (yet still reasonably affordable), and attract more legacy students than public HBCUs. However, public HBCUs enroll approximately 76% of all students attending HBCUs. Overwhelmingly, HBCUs (approximately 89%) are in the southern states (NCES, 2020).

The HBCU Experience

The value and appeal of HBCUs are unmatched. Often Black students select HBCUs to be surrounded by people with similar backgrounds and racial experiences and to be a part of rich cultural history (Saunders & Nagle, 2018). However, a focus on Black students does not mean a limited cultural experience for any of the students who attend. HBCUs serve students from a wide range of racial, cultural, socioeconomic, and international backgrounds at both the undergraduate and graduate levels and enroll a significant percentage of students who go on to graduate and professional schools. Additionally, the majority of HBCUs have a more racially diverse faculty and administration than PWIs. In 2018, 24% of enrollment at HBCUs was from non-Black students (NCES, 2020).

Perhaps what sets HBCUs apart from other institutions is the student experience. According to a 2015 Gallup poll, there was a 'thriving gap' identified between Black graduates of HBCUs and Black graduates of other types of institutions (*e.g.*, predominately White institutions) (Seymour & Ray, 2015). Black HBCU graduates, compared to Black graduates of PWIs, were more likely to report higher levels of thriving in five key areas of well-being: purpose, social, financial, community, and physical. Of the five areas of well-being, HBCU graduates demonstrated higher percentages of thriving in purpose and social well-being. Black HBCU graduates indicated stronger feelings of support while they were on campus, more experiential learning opportunities in college, and being better prepared for life after graduation. One of the largest reported gaps in the poll between HBCU and non-HBCU Black graduates was in feelings of 'being cared for by professors.' HBCUs are widely known for having an institutional climate that is supportive, nurturing, and family-like. Freeman et al. (2021) conducted a large qualitative study with 212 Black students to ascertain their HBCU experiences and found three major themes: 1) institutional culture, 2) culturally relevant pedagogy, and 3) positive faculty-student interaction. One student noted, *"I feel that the greatest value of attending a historically Black university is the close-knit family environment that the campus provides"* (p.5). These institutions provide environments that are seen as counternarratives to predominate negative stereotypes and biases about Black people that are widespread in society.

For the Culture

HBCUs are historically rooted in racial pride and social justice, and the Mission statements of most HBCUs reflect their collectivistic values, practices, and the importance of community service and support.

They occupy a distinct space for Black people, their families, and their communities. Students are immersed in culturally relevant pedagogy by faculty who are invested in the success of Black students and committed to participating in what some may consider being a "high-touch environment." High-touch environments are those that emphasize experiential learning opportunities for students, as well as high levels of student engagement. Williams et al. (2021) examined pedagogy and educational practices of HBCU faculty members and administrators and noted the various ways in which environments are created that prioritize validation, center the experiences of Black communities inside and outside of the classroom, and create learning spaces where Blackness is a central element in the knowledge generation and discovery processes.

Beginning in the 1980s, the culture of HBCUs made its way to the mainstream media through movies, television shows, and more recently, music concerts and venues. Generation X'ers (1965–1980) had the pleasure of witnessing one of the most impactful movies focused on the culture of Black colleges, *School Daze*. Writer and Director Spike Lee brought all the beauty, and some of the drama of HBCU culture and life to the big screen in 1988. The movie touched upon salient, historical issues for the Black community that were still relevant during that time period. The movie did not just focus on the Black community in the US, but the global community as a way of expressing the principle of Ubuntu – *"I am because we are, and we are because I am."* In 121 minutes, poignant issues impacting the global Black community such as prejudice and discrimination, colorism, classism, apartheid in South Africa, and sexuality were brought to life with an HBCU as the backdrop. Five years after *School Daze*, a television show that would introduce mainstream audiences to the HBCU experience, *A Different World* (1993) debuted. Each week audiences experienced diverse, unforgettable characters such as Whitley Gilbert, Dwayne Wayne, Denise Huxtable, and Freddie Brooks navigate the inevitable collegiate transitions at a fictional HBCU. For many viewers, this was their first experience with HBCUs and seeing Black college students on television. Since *A Different World*, there have been a handful of movies (*Drumline, Stomp the Yard, The Great Debaters*) that illuminate various factions of the HBCU culture for not just Black students but for all students in attendance. Additionally, these representations included the relationships between students, faculty, and staff. One of the hallmarks of HBCUs is the 'family atmosphere' that welcomes and supports students. In 2004, a reality show, *College Hill*, debuted on Black Entertainment Television (BET). College Hill was a show that followed the lives of students who attended HBCUs. During the six seasons the show was on the network, students from HBCUs such as Southern University (Louisiana), Langston University (Oklahoma), Virginia State University (Virginia), University of the Virgin Islands (Virgin Islands), and two HBCUs in Atlanta, Georgia (Clark Atlanta University and Morehouse College) talked about and gave a glimpse into their HBCU culture. BET saw some record numbers of viewership posted during these years, and the interest and intrigue of HBCUs continued. In 2017, *The Quad* debuted on BET and followed the newly elected first female president of a fictional HBCU, Georgia A&M University. The show was designed to hold space for a discussion of the intersection of race, gender, power, and privilege on university campuses. In each HBCU representation, there was criticism regarding the portrayal of the culture. Was it accurate? Did 'they' expose too much information? Would people think about HBCUs after viewing?

More recently, 'The Culture,' was represented by none other than the one they call 'Queen Bey,' Beyoncé. In 2018, she brought an enormous amount of positive attention to HBCUs and the beloved HBCU culture to many who were unfamiliar with it. As the first Black woman to headline the worldwide phenomenon known as Coachella, the hashtag #Beychella was born. Her performance, *Homecoming*, was seen by many around the world on Netflix as an ode to the HBCU experience. Although she did not attend an HBCU, she centered some of the most storied traditions and cultural representations of HBCUs in her performance, such as the Marching Band, dancers and majorettes, and 'stepping' by fraternities and sororities. She was able to capture the overall spirit of an HBCU homecoming.

The next chapter delves a little deeper into HBCUs and how the unique cultural and contextual environments are related to the sexual attitudes, beliefs, decision-making, expression, and behavior of young Black college students.

References

Association of Public & Land-grant Universities (n.d.). *Council of 1890s Institutions.* https://www.aplu.org/members/councils/1890-universities/council-of-1890s-institutions.html

Buhi, E. R., Marhefka, S. L., & Hoban, M. T. (2010). The state of the union: Sexual health disparities in a national sample of US college students. *Journal of American College Health, 58*(4), 337–346. 10.1080/07448480903501780

Centers for Disease Control and Prevention. (2019, June). *Sexual Health.* National Center for HIV/AIDS, Viral Hepatitis, STD, and TB Prevention. https://www.cdc.gov/sexualhealth/Default.html

Freeman, K. E., Winston-Proctor, C. E., Gangloff-Bailey, F., & Jones, J. M. (2021). Racial identity-rooted academic motivation of first-year African American students majoring in STEM at an HBCU. *Frontiers in Psychology, 12.*

Hogben, M., Harper, C., Habel, M. A., Brookmeyer, K., & Friedman, A. (2017). Attitudes to sexual health in the United States: Results from a national survey of youth aged 15-25 years. *Sexual Health, 14*(6), 540–547. 10.1071/SH16164

Ladson-Billings, G. (1995). Toward a theory of culturally relevant pedagogy. *American Educational Research Journal, 32*(3), 465–491.

National Center for Education Statistics (2016). Digest of education statistics: 2016. Retrieved from https://nces.ed.gov/ipeds/

National Center for Education Statistics. (2020). *Integrated Postsecondary Education Data System* (IPEDS), *"Fall Enrollment Survey"* (IPEDS-EF:90). https://nces.ed.gov/programs/digest/d19/tables/dt19_313.30.asp

Office of the Surgeon General (US), Office of Population Affairs (2021, July). *The Surgeon General's Call to Action to Promote Sexual Health and Responsible Sexual Behavior.* Rockville (MD): Office of the Surgeon General (US). Available from: https://www.ncbi.nlm.nih.gov/books/NBK44216/

Saunders, K. M., & Nagle, B. T. (2018). HBCUs punching above their weight: A state-level analysis of Historically Black College and University enrollment and graduation. *Frederick D. Patterson Research Institute, United Negro College Fund.*

Seymour, S., & Ray, J. (2015). Grads of historically black colleges have well-being edge. *Gallup. com, 1127.* Retrieved from: https://www.npr.org/templates/story/story.php?storyId=16069645.

Thurgood Marshall College Fund (2019). *About PBIs.* Retrieved from: https://www.tmcf.org/about-us/member-schools/about-pbis/

Thurstone, L. L. (1931). The measurement of social attitudes. *The Journal of Abnormal and Social Psychology, 26*(3), 249.

U.S. Department of Education, Office for Civil Rights (1991). *Historically Black Colleges and Universities and higher education desegregation.* Retrieved from: https://www2.ed.gov/about/offices/list/ocr/docs/hq9511.html

Williams, K. L., Russell, A., & Summerville, K. (2021). Centering Blackness: An examination of culturally affirming pedagogy and practices enacted by HBCU administrators and faculty members. *Innovative Higher Education, 46*(6), 733–757.

World Health Organization. (2015). *Sexual health, human rights and the law.* World Health Organization.

Younge, S. N., Boyer, C. B., Geter, A., Barker, J. C., & Corneille, M. (2014). An exploration of the sexual behaviors of emerging adult men attending a historically Black College/University. *Journal of Black Sexuality and Relationships, 1*(1), 65.

Younge, S. N., Corneille, M. A., Lyde, M., & Cannady, J. (2013). The paradox of risk: Historically Black college/university students and sexual health. *Journal of American College Health, 61*(5), 254–262.

Younge, S. N., Wade, B. H., Geter, A., Holliday, R. C., & Trawick, C. (2018). Condom attitudes and condom use among first year college men attending a historically Black institution. *American Journal of Health Studies, 33*(2), 80–88.

2 HBCUs and Sexual Health: The Importance of Culture and Context

The importance of examining sexual health among young Black college students cannot be overstated. As mentioned in Chapter 1, sexual health is as valuable to your overall well-being as any other type of health, yet it is often neglected because there may be ambivalent or negative emotions such as shame, fear, confusion, embarrassment, and/or anger associated with it. As a society, we have not fully embraced the sexual aspects of ourselves. Sexuality is fundamental to overall health and well-being. Although everyone must contend with aspects of their sexual health, this does not prevent people from projecting their issues with sexuality and sexual behavior onto others. The messages communicated to us, either directly or indirectly, about sexual health from people we respect help construct our identities as sexual beings (Rubinsky & Cooke-Johnson, 2017). In an article written for *Psychology Today*, Schafer (2010) wrote "words cannot change reality, but they can change how people perceive reality." We create our reality by language, labels, and categories that are assigned to thoughts, feelings, and behaviors that we have versus those that others have. How we label (or stigmatize) people and behaviors uncover how we allow our biases and prejudices to be cast upon others. Labeling, or naming, specifies what something suggests and how it should be treated by the person labeling it and others (Zamani-Gallaher, 2017). For example, the use of words like 'natural' vs. 'unnatural,' or 'normal' vs. 'abnormal' or even 'nasty,' are powerful in that they set the stage for processing and incorporating information into our schemas. Schemas are rules used to categorize and interpret the world. Markus (1977) viewed 'schemas' as ways in which we organize information about ourselves which are derived from past experiences, current experiences, and how we facilitate the processing of information. Almost 20 years later, Andersen and Cyranowski (1994) introduced the concept, *sexual self-schema*, which was operationalized as cognitive generalizations about sexual aspects of oneself. Our sexual self-schemas are thought to provide the information

DOI: 10.4324/9781003180944-2

(or foundation) for the enactment of scripts for future behavioral responses in sexual situations and relationships. These sexual scripts are posited to cue certain sexual attitudes, beliefs, and experiences in situations. Sexual schemas are formed from personal sexual behavior, sexual emotions, and arousal, and help to frame current experience and guide current inferences about all aspects of sexual health. A small body of research on the sexual schemas and scripts of Black people is available but almost solely focuses on adolescents or adults. More research needs to be done with Black college-aged individuals because they are at a point in development where sexual attitudes, values, and habits are being developed and shaped. Since sexual self-views are likely to change as one progresses through transitional phases, it is important to investigate psychosocial and sociocultural variables relevant to how young people cognitively conceptualize themselves as sexual beings.

The WHO noted that *"for sexual health to be attained and maintained, the sexual rights of all persons must be respected, protected and fulfilled"* (World Health Organization, 2015, *p. 5*). Good overall sexual health requires knowledge and understanding of various aspects of one's sexual self, feeling comfortable with it, and celebrating it. This may be an easy task for some, but many people spend their entire lives trying to reconcile multiple aspects of their sexuality and sexual health. It is quite challenging for many to be comfortable with their sexual identity, societal norms for dress and behavior, or their sexual desires for certain types of activities or pleasure. If sexual health and all it encompasses is difficult for many individuals in their mid and late adulthood stages, imagine how challenging it is for young people to navigate. College students have a low perceived risk for poor health outcomes, in general, and perhaps sexual health outcomes specifically. They often fall victim to the '*Not Me*' fallacy and believe that undesirable consequences and outcomes will not be their fate, irrespective of the decisions they make and/or the risks they take. Since young Black college students have poorer sexual health outcomes than college students of other racial/ethnic groups (Younge et al., 2018), it is imperative to investigate the culture and context of where a significant portion of our Black college students spend time working on their personal and professional development.

The Sexual Milieu of HBCUs

The sexual milieu, or environment, of Black college students, is an area where more culturally and ecologically relevant, and responsive, research is necessary. College is not only an educational transitional period but also a cultural, social, and ecological transition. Bronfenbrenner (1979) defines an ecological transition as *"occurring whenever a person's position in the ecological environment is altered as a result of a change in role, setting, or both"* (p. 26). The period from entering as a freshman to graduate, typically, is the developmental period (18–29 years) called *emerging adulthood* (Arnett, 2000). The sexual and reproductive health of students cannot be understood outside of the cultural context of the HBCUs they attend. For many students, the college environment provides a sense of newfound freedom, self-determination, and peer pressure to engage in risky behavior, including sexual risk behavior. During this time, individual experiences increase vulnerability to poorer sexual decision-making and overall sexual health outcomes. The changes, both developmentally and ecologically, begin to happen as soon as students step onto the college campus. Students are met with new people, new rules, new expectations, and new opportunities. How one decides *who? what? when? where? why?* and *how?* becomes more important as one acclimate to a new culture. These critical shifts can have profound short- and long-term consequences on an individual's psychological, emotional, and physical well-being.

Campus Culture

College students, irrespective of sociodemographic characteristics, are subject to similar psychological, social, and cultural experiences during their college years. Evidence demonstrates that the unique social environment or *culture* of the campus is related to sexual health outcomes for students (Adefuye et al., 2009). Many researchers believe culture is a particularly salient contextual factor in sexual health (Airhihenbuwa et al., 1992; Jemmott et al., 1995). Essentially, culture is a life-affirming code of behavior that supports existence (Bracey, 2002; Pequegnat & Stover, 1999). According to the American Sexual Health Association (2021), each culture and subculture has its own standards of sexual health. Therefore, attitudes about sexual health, sexuality, roles, norms, and behaviors are deeply rooted in the culture and history of individuals, their relationships, and where they live.

  HBCUs offer an important lens through which researchers can further explore how young Black college students understand, experience, and prioritize their sexual health. A unique characteristic about HBCUs that may be critical when discussing sexual health is that they often serve as a microcosm of the larger Black community. HBCUs are often geographically located within Black communities (Treadwell, et al., 2009) and have many similarities and challenges documented in broader psychological, social, and cultural contexts. Research indicates that HBCU students commonly have sexual partners who are of the same race and/or ethnicity (Hall & Applewhite, 2013; Younge et al., 2014) and are often not students but live in the surrounding area (Younge et al., 2007). This may increase the risk for poorer sexual health outcomes such as acquiring and transmitting STIs, including HIV from potential/actual sexual partners because of the high prevalence in the surrounding communities. HBCUs have been characterized as a 'bridge' between low- and high-risk populations (Hightow et al., 2005; Younge et al., 2013) due to the high proportion of students who engage in sexual activity on and off-campus. Given the trend toward assortative mixing and the disparate STI and HIV disease burden in areas where many HBCUs are located, stronger public health messages targeting young Black college-age youth should fill gaps in knowledge regarding contexts of risk (LeBlanc et al., 2014).

There is a misconception that college students are not vulnerable to many of the ills in society as they are protected from the outside world because they live or spend a great deal of time on campus. There are certain protections afforded to students that shield them from outside influences while they are matriculating. This may be the case with some institutions, but HBCUs, in general, are located within the local communities that are grappling with economic and social oppression. Additionally, many of the poorer sexual health outcomes (e.g., unplanned pregnancies, STI, and HIV rates) are among Black people living in southern states, which is where the vast majority of HBCUs are located. An important question to ask is whether campus culture acts as a protective factor, or if it helps to facilitate risky behavior for students? Realistically, it can be both and should be explored in more depth.

While it has been documented that those with higher levels of education are correlated with better health outcomes, this positive correlation is not as pronounced in young Black college students (Chandler et al., 2021) as it is in other populations. Interestingly, Black HBCU students report specific protective factors at similar or higher rates than students at predominately White institutions (PWIs), yet still bear a disproportionate burden of disparate sexual health outcomes (Hou, 2009; Sutton et al., 2011). For example, HBCU students are less likely to suffer from substance abuse (Hall & Jones, 2020; Younge et al., 2013) but are more likely to have an earlier age of sexual debut (Wang et al., 2011). A better understanding of the sexual milieu of Black college students at HBCUs is needed to help guide the development of strategies and interventions to improve sexual health outcomes and advance the translation of culturally grounded research into effective practice.

Black students attending HBCUs have always represented cultural diversity in ways beyond race and ethnicity. As more diverse groups of students enter HBCUs, there will be inevitable cultural shifts taking place. Some of these cultural swings are welcomed with open arms and others are met with more hesitation. Many HBCUs are enjoying the growing number of students from different racial and ethnic groups, religions, socioeconomic statuses, and an increase in international student enrollment. Contrarily, as people are exploring gender and sexual diversity at earlier ages than many of the faculty, staff, and alumni did, more students are using their wardrobe, hair, and even social media to express themselves in ways that may be uncomfortable for some established campus cultures. There have been some publicized 'incidents' on HBCU campuses that have garnered national attention. Some are seen as progressive, such as the decision by Spelman College (an all-female HBCU in Atlanta) in 2017 to 'accept transgender women into the college.' It is not clear whether transgender women were not 'allowed' before the decision, but the Admissions policy was changed to reflect this inclusive language. Morehouse College (an all-male HBCU neighboring Spelman College) followed suit in 2019 and opened its enrollment to transgender men. These two examples are bringing attention to the various social and sexual identities that young Black students are embracing and celebrating. As more young people move away from the socially constructed gender and sexual binary labels, the administration, and governing Boards at HBCUs must decide whether they will flow with the changing sociodemographic of the students, or if they will stand steadfast to tradition and rules that may be more exclusive than inclusive. The million-dollar question is whether HBCUs are equipped to not only welcome and graduate these students but support them in ways that help them thrive on campus and beyond. Although the answer may seem as easy as a *yes* or *no,* it is not. Institutions of higher education answer to a governing Board of Trustees or Directors, and in the case of publicly funded HBCUs, to some degree the taxpayers. They are bound by different rules, regulations, and oversight than privately funded HBCUs and much of what gets adopted and implemented is a delicate political dance. As Offices of Enrollment Management develop recruitment plans for Generation Z students, they must plan for diverse student populations who will challenge them to create spaces that celebrate and support them.

The HBCU Context

HBCUs are bastions of Black excellence and innovation (Albritton, 2012). This is seen from the centering of people in the African diaspora in pedagogy and activities to the uplift of racial pride, and the familial environment that emphasizes 'high-touch between faculty, staff, and student.' High touch is a student-centered method that involves hands-on approaches to teaching, learning, and engagement. While there are numerous variables crucial to understanding the sexual milieu of Black college students at HBCUs, two are highlighted early in the book because of their relative importance to the overall experience on HBCU campuses. Whether or not one considers themselves religious, it is no secret that religion, more specifically, the Black Church is an ever-present influence on many HBCU campuses. Another mainstay for HBCU campuses is the issue of respectability politics and what they represent and regulate. Below are brief overviews of how these two elements of HBCUs have a profound influence on the sexual health and environment of Black college students.

Religion

Religion historically has been an important part of Black life in the United States. Whether or not one is religious may be less important than the undeniable history of the Black Church as a beacon of light in dark days for many Black individuals and families. This is the case for many of the older HBCUs which have a long, storied history with churches (Black and White) and missionary groups. The American Missionary Association (AMA), the Freedmen's Bureau, and several denominations helped to establish numerous HBCUs such as Hampton University (formerly Institute), Fisk University, and Dillard University. Much like the premise of religious and service organizations, HBCUs see social justice, morality, character development, community service, and servant leadership as cornerstones to their mission and purpose. Additionally, HBCUs are commonly considered to be institutions founded on ideas of political and religious conservatism. While some of the principles of religious institutions may still be important in the lives of young Black college students, it would be neglectful to not acknowledge activities like church attendance have declining significance to many young Black college students. Through personal experience as a long-time faculty member at an HBCU, students appreciate the doctrine availed to them by religion but not necessarily the perceived restrictions. Many private HBCUs have a chapel, sometimes non-denominational, on-site, and still require attendance at religious-themed activities and events for continued enrollment. For example, Oakwood University (Huntsville, Alabama) is a historically Black Seventh-day Adventist institution, and any student taking over six credit hours is required to attend weekly chapel/assemblies (Oakwood University, 2019). Even with less identification of being 'religious,' religion still plays a critical role in the life of many Black HBCU students. Given that most HBCUs were founded with strong ties to religious institutions, an important characteristic to explore in this population is the influence of religion on their overall sexual health. Religion and sexual health are inevitably linked through beliefs, attitudes, knowledge, and ultimately, behavior. Oftentimes those who identify as more religious have more 'conservative' views on sexuality, sexual expression, and sexual behavior. It can be viewed as a code of conduct that acts as a compass for sexual norms and behaviors (Spadt et al., 2014). But also, there is a positive correlation between being more religious and accepting of patriarchy, male dominance, traditional gender role adherence, heterosexism, and homophobia (Johnson, 2017). Returning to the question posed previously about HBCUs and welcoming and supporting students whose beliefs may be different than those of the dominant culture on campus. Are they ready to accept that people can have a religious foundation and still express their sexuality in diverse ways? Although there can be some laymen theories about the relationship between religion and sexuality and behavior, the empirical research for Black college students at HBCUs is mixed. This area is explored more in the *Psychosocial Influences on Sexual Health* section (Chapter 5).

Politics of Respectability

The term *respectability politics* is used to describe established rules by which people from marginalized groups police their own member's behaviors to be more in alignment with dominant values (Harris, 2014). Higginbotham (1993) coined the term *politics of Black respectability* and defines it as the promotion of cleanliness, polite manners, self-restraint, sexual purity, and frugality to disrupt negative perceptions of Black people. Black American institutions (*e.g.*, family, church, schools) created and still maintain the guidelines of respectable behavior of Black Americans. Historically, respectability politics served as a survival mechanism to mitigate experiences of racial prejudice and discrimination. Leaders in the Black community wanted to dismantle negative stereotypes seen in the media and throughout society about Black Americans through appearance, success, and achievement. These policies dictate what is deemed 'appropriate' for faculty, staff, and students, and to some degree, outline preferred performances of gender and sexuality (Njoku et al., 2017). While there is a fair amount of criticism thrown at these policies and rules, it must be acknowledged that they were created to transform the perception of Black Americans, and in fact, could have quite possibly been the difference between life or death for many. The original intent was not to be restrictive or oppressive but to help create better environments for Black Americans who were existing in times where the color of their skin made it unsafe to just 'be.' This notwithstanding, there are some who believe the protection it was designed to afford has created 'othering' narratives that are rooted in classism, elitism, and the belief that these practices will shield one from the reality of racism and the myth of White supremacy (Njoku et al., 2017). Additionally, the villainization of certain aesthetics and behaviors, particularly those related to gender and sexual identity and expression, may be seen as excluding certain forms of Black identity. Are there certain factions of Black identity that are not acceptable at HBCUs?

Ideologies of respectability politics surrounding appearance are being supported and reinforced on the campuses of some HBCUs. Hampton University (Hampton, Virginia) is well-known for its dress code that is based on "the theory that learning to use socially acceptable manners and selecting attire appropriate to specific occasions and activities is critical factors in the educational process" (Hampton University, n.d.) According to the university website,

> "All administrative, faculty and support staff members will be expected to monitor student behavior applicable to this dress code and report any such disregard or violations to the Offices of the Dean of Men, or Dean of Women for the attention of the Vice President for Student Affairs."

In 2007, in response to Hampton University banning cornrows or dreadlocks in their MBA program, President Michael Sorrell of Paul Quinn College (Dallas, TX) acknowledged that "historically Black colleges have a history of expecting a certain level of dress as a way of preparing the students to combat the stereotypes which we know we all face" (Martin, 11/7/2007). In the Oakwood University Student Handbook, a description of 'Christian Dress' is provided, "The principles of modesty, chastity, simplicity, propriety, good taste, neatness, comeliness, and consistent witness are core values that relate to Christian dress. Biblical guidelines for modesty do not depend on current fashion trends." If one reads further, much of the Dress Code is related to the Oakwood Woman, with only a small entry for men that emphasizes inappropriate headgear (e.g., durags, stocking caps, hats) for men. To be clear, it is not unusual for educational institutions to have dress code policies; however, the enforcement of the dress codes appears to receive more attention at HBCUs (Hall et al., 2020) and many theorize that it is based on a history of respectability politics.

Some HBCU campuses may dictate student's expressions and performances through dress codes, thus creating a discriminatory climate for sexual freedom and non-binary gender identification (Harper & Gasman, 2008; Njoku et al., 2017). Mobley and Hall (2020) note that Black students who identify as queer and/or transgender are often overlooked at HBCUs due to the complexities of their intersecting sexual and gender identity with their chosen gender expression(s). If a student meets all the criteria to attend the university but does not identify as *He* or *She*, but *They*, where do *they* fit in? There appears to be a generational divide in the understanding and support for respectability politics at HBCUs. Often this gap is between HBCU administrators and Black youth activists, on some campuses, who are committed to combating social and political issues impacting the Black community. For example, Betsy DeVos, the United States Secretary of Education (2017–2021) was invited to be the commencement speaker at Bethune Cookman University (Daytona Beach, FL) graduation in 2017. Some graduating students booed and turned their backs while she delivered her remarks and when she was awarded an honorary doctorate. President Edison Jackson issued a warning to the students to 'sit down' or 'have their degrees mailed to them.' The incident provoked discussions in the media, on social media, and at the dinner table about how Black students should behave in Black communities, for White people to feel relaxed.

Some HBCUs, and departments within the institutions maintain strict codes of conduct and if students disobey these, they may lose certain privileges or may be subject to expulsion (Ihle, 1992). Guy-Sheftall and Cole (2003) note the intersection of gender and race and insist that though all HBCU students are subject to rules identified within the campus code of conduct, HBCUs often have more restrictive rules for Black women that are implemented to guide, protect, and develop them into respectable women. The dress code was one way identified to oversee, or some would say 'to police' student bodies. Some of the restrictive gendered rules mentioned by Guy-Sheftall and Cole are seen as high up the administrative ladder as the President or Chancellor of the university. In 2013, Alabama State University (Montgomery, Alabama) hired Dr. Gwendolyn Boyd, an alumna, as its first female president. The Board of Trustees had a stipulation in her contract that was dubbed 'the love clause' by media outlets (Dimitrova, 2014). Her contract specified that "for as long as Dr. Boyd is President and a single person, she shall not be allowed to cohabitate in the President's residence with any person with whom she has a romantic relation." This raised eyebrows for several reasons, one of which is the belief that regulating one's romantic and sexual life is out of bounds for an employer. Additionally, was this type of regulation a standard clause in previous presidential contracts for males?

While HBCUs deliver high-quality educational experiences for students, often on shoestring budgets, there are still areas that need further exploration and improvement. While religion and respectability politics have roots in positivity for the Black community, there are limitations. The ideology surrounding may be steeped in the desire to minimize stigma and discrimination, but the practices and application may need to be reimagined. As stated by the opening quote, the sexual rights of all persons must be respected, protected, and fulfilled. For HBCUs to remain spaces of liberation and transformation, it requires the courage to not be complicit or accept the status quo, and to continue pursuing social justice for all students. As a start, it is important to understand the reproductive and sexual health landscape for young Black college students. The next chapter provides an overview of important and available statistical information related to this topic.

References

Adefuye, A. S., Abiona, T. C., Balogun, J. A., & Lokoro-Durrell, M. (2009). HIV sexual risk behaviors and perception of risk among college students: Implications for planning interventions. *BMC Public Health, 9*(1), 1–13.

Airhihenbuwa, C., DiClemente, R., Wingood, G., & Lowe, A. (1992). HIV/AIDS Education and Prevention among African Americans: A focus on culture. *AIDS Education and Prevention, 4*, 267–276.

Albritton, T. J. (2012). Educating our own: The historical legacy of HBCUs and their relevance for educating a new generation of leaders. *The Urban Review, 44*(3), 311–331.

American Sexual Health Association (2021, May 26). *Understanding Sexual Health.* https://www.ashasexualhealth.org/sexual-health/

Andersen, B. L., & Cyranowski, J. M. (1994). Women's sexual self-schema. *Journal of Personality and Social Psychology, 67*(6), 1079.

Arnett, J. J. (2000). Emerging adulthood: A theory of development from the late teens through the twenties. *American Psychologist, 55*(5), 469.

Bracey, J. M. (2002, September). *What the heck is cultural competency for African Americans?* Paper presented at United Conference on AIDS, Anaheim, CA.

Bronfenbrenner, U. (1979). *The ecology of human development: Experiments by nature and design.* Cambridge, MA: Harvard University Press.

Chandler, R., Guillaume, D., Tesema, N., Paul, S., Ross, H., & Hernandez, N. D. (2021). Social and environmental influences on sexual behaviors of college Black women: Within group diversity between HBCU vs. PWI experiences. *Journal of Racial and Ethnic Health Disparities, 8*(4), 852–862.

Dimitrova, K. (2014, January 10). '*Love Clause; appears in contract of college president.*' *ABC News.* https://abcnews.go.com/US/love-clause-appears-contract-college-president/story?id=21494543

Guy-Sheftall, B., & Cole, J. B. (2003). *Gender talk: The struggle for women's equality in African American communities.* New York: Random House.

Hall, N. M., & Applewhite, S. (2013). Masculine ideology, norms, and HIV prevention among young Black men. *Journal of HIV/AIDS & Social Services, 12,* 384–403.

Hall, N. M., Dickens, D., Lee, A. K., Corneille, M., & Younge, S. N. (2020). Colorism and racial politics at Historically Black Colleges/Universities. In K. Woodson (Ed.), *Colorism then, now, & tomorrow: Redefining a global phenomenon, with implications for policy, research, and practice.* Santa Barbara, CA: Fielding University Press.

Hall, N. M., & Jones, J. M. (2020). Predictors of sexual risk among HBCU students: Implications for STI/HIV prevention and intervention. *Journal of Black Sexuality and Relationships, 6*(3), 71–92.

Hampton University (n.d.). *Student Life: Dress Code.* https://www.hamptonu.edu/student_life/dresscode.cfm.

Harper, S. R. & Gasman, M. (2008). Consequences of conservatism: Black male undergraduates and the politics of Historically Black Colleges and Universities. *The Journal of Negro Education, 77*(4), 336–351.

Harris, F. C. (2014). The rise of respectability politics. *Dissent, 61*(1), 33–37.

Higginbotham, E. B. (1993). The politics of respectability. *Righteous discontent: The women's movement in the Black Baptist church, 1880–1920,* 185–230.

Hightow, L. B., MacDonald, P. D., Pilcher, C. D., Kaplan, A. H., Foust, E., Nguyen, T. Q., & Leone, P. A. (2005). The unexpected movement of the HIV epidemic in the Southeastern United States: Transmission among college students. *JAIDS Journal of Acquired Immune Deficiency Syndromes, 38*(5), 531–537.

Hou, S. I. (2009). HIV-related behaviors among black students attending Historically Black Colleges and Universities (HBCUs) versus white students attending a traditionally white institution (TWI). *AIDS Care, 21*(8), 1050–1057.

Ihle, E. L. (1992). *Black women in higher education: An anthology of essays, studies, and documents* (Vol. 2). Taylor & Francis.

Jemmott, J. S., Catan, V., Nyamathi, A., & Anastasia, J. (1995). African American women and HIV-risk-reduction issues. In: A. O'Leary & L. S. Jemmott (Eds.), *Women at risk: Issues in the primary prevention of AIDS.* New York, NY: Plenum Press.

Johnson, J. M. (2017). Social norms, gender ratio imbalance, perceptions of risk, and the sexual behaviors of African American women at Historically Black Colleges and Universities. *Journal of African American Studies, 21,* 203–215. 10.1007/s12111-017-9354-8

LeBlanc, T. T., Sutton, M. Y., Thomas, P., & Duffus, W. A. (2014). HIV and STI risk for young Blacks in high prevalence areas: Implication for health equity in communities hosting historically Black colleges and universities (HBCUs). *Journal of Health Disparities Research and Practice, 7*(1).

Markus, H. (1977). Self-schemata and processing information about the self. *Journal of Personality and Social Psychology, 35*(2), 63.

Martin, M. (Host). (2007, November 7). HBCU president enforces strict dress code [Radio broadcast episode]. https://www.npr.org/templates/story/story.php?storyId=16069645.

Mobley Jr, S. D., & Hall, L. (2020). (Re) Defining queer and trans* student retention and "success" at Historically Black Colleges and Universities. *Journal of College Student Retention: Research, Theory & Practice, 21*(4), 497–519.

Njoku, N., Butler, M., & Beatty, C. C. (2017). Reimagining the historically Black college and university (HBCU) environment: Exposing race secrets and the binding chains of respectability and othermothering. *International Journal of Qualitative Studies in Education, 30*(8), 783–799.

Oakwood University (2019). *Student Handbook: Academic Year 2019–2020.* https://www2.oakwood.edu/wp-content/uploads/Student-Handbook_-rev.-2-18-2020-1.pdf

Pequegnat, W., & Stover, E. (1999). Considering women's contextual and cultural issues in HIV/STD prevention research. *Cultural Diversity and Ethnic Minority Psychology, 5*, 287–291.

Rubinsky, V., & Cooke-Johnson, A. (2017). "Tell me something other than to use a condom and sex is scary": Memorable messages whom and gender minorities wish for and recall about sexual health. *Women's Studies in Communication, 40*(4), 379–400.

Schafer, J. (November, 2010). Words have power. Retrieved from: https://www.psychologytoday.com/us/blog/let-their-words-do-the-talking/201011/words-have-power.

Spadt, S. K., Rosenbaum, T. Y., Dweck, A., Millheiser, L., Pillai-Friedman, S., & Krychman, M. (2014). CME information: Sexual health and religion: A primer for the sexual health clinician (CME). *The Journal of Sexual Medicine, 11*(7), 1606–1619.

Sutton, M. Y., Hardnett, F. P., Wright, P., Wahi, S., Pathak, S., Warren-Jeanpiere, L., & Jones, S. (2011). HIV/AIDS knowledge scores and perceptions of risk among African American students attending historically black colleges and universities. *Public Health Reports, 126*(5), 653–663.

Treadwell, H. M., Braithwaite, R. L., Braithwaite, K., Oliver, D., & Holliday, R. (2009). Leadership development for health researchers at historically Black colleges and universities. *American Journal of Public Health, 99*(S1), S53–S57.

Wang, Y., Storr, C., Browne, D. C., & Wagner, F. A. (2011). Early sexual experience and later onset of illegal drug use among African American students on HBCU campuses. *Substance Use & Misuse, 46*(4), 543–551.

World Health Organization. (2015). *Sexual health, human rights and the law.* World Health Organization.

Younge, S. N., Boyer, C. B., Geter, A., Barker, J. C., & Corneille, M. (2014). An exploration of the sexual behaviors of emerging adult men attending a historically Black College/University. *Journal of Black Sexuality and Relationships, 1*(1), 65.

Younge, S. N., Corneille, M. A., Lyde, M., & Cannady, J. (2013). The paradox of risk: Historically Black college/university students and sexual health. *Journal of American College Health, 61*(5), 254–262.

Younge, S. N., Smith, D., Young, L., Cole, D., Reynolds, L., Dixon, R., ... & Buchanan, P. N. (2007). Intersection between race, gender, and sexual risk: Implications for STI/HIV on HBCU campuses. *Challenge Online, 13*(2), 37–60.

Younge, S. N., Wade, B. H., Geter, A., Holliday, R. C., & Trawick, C. (2018). Condom attitudes and condom use among first year college men attending a historically Black institution. *American Journal of Health Studies, 33*(2), 80–88.

Zamani-Gallaher, E. M. (2017). Conflating gender and identity: The need for gender-fluid programming in community colleges. *New Directions for Community Colleges, 2017*(179), 89–99.

3 The State of Black College Students' Sexual Health

Much like the annual Presidential *State of the Union address*, this chapter provides information on the current state of sexual health among young Black college-aged students. This chapter introduces, and brief overview of, available statistical information on sexual health behaviors, outcomes, and disparities of young Black men and women in the United States.

Sexual Health

Sexual health disparities among Black college-aged individuals are based on a combination of factors that include knowledge, attitudes, perceptions, environmental influences, behaviors, lack of access to accurate information and services, and structural factors such as poverty, racism, sexism, and discrimination. Disparities are defined by the differences in the disease and the related adverse health conditions that exist among specific groups within the population and are measured by the following epidemiological measures:

- Incidence – the number of new cases in a population over a specified period
- Prevalence – the number of all existing cases in a population over a specified period
- Mortality – the number of deaths in a population over a specified period

In this short chapter, an introduction to and overview of, reproductive and sexual health statistics are presented. As one may imagine, disparities in sexual and reproductive health outcomes are disturbingly higher than many other areas of health (Ford et al., 2017). The Centers for Disease Control and Prevention (CDC) provide statistics on the

DOI: 10.4324/9781003180944-3

following sexual health topics and outcomes, often stratified by race/ethnicity, gender, age, and sexual orientation:

- *Reproductive health*: includes contraceptive use, pregnancy and birth data, and women's health
- *Sexual violence*: includes intimate partner violence (IPV) and sex trafficking
- *Sexual risk behavior* includes infectious diseases, such as STIs and HIV/AIDs

An important note about the sexual health data reported. The most current data from the American College Health Association (ACHA), which focuses on the health behaviors and outcomes of college students in the United States, is not included in this chapter. Unfortunately, based on the spring 2019 report (American College Health Association, 2019), less than 5% of the participants identified as Black or African American, and no students from HBCUs were participants in the dataset. Therefore, the most current data comes from a variety of other national sources.

Statistical Overview

Reproductive Health

Taking care of one's reproductive health includes making decisions about contraception, safer sex practices, and access to culturally affirming, effective, and affordable care (American Sexual Health Association, 2021). Each individual needs to understand their needs, beliefs, perspectives, values, and options so they can make the best decision possible. Throughout the chapters, Black college students are repeatedly discussed as having the desire to avoid unplanned pregnancy as the impact on their lives is immediate and long-term. The effects of STIs, including HIV can be as immediate and long-term as pregnancies, yet the perspective and belief about impact make students choose certain safer sex practices over others. Nationally, the birth rate for Black, non-Hispanic mothers (ages 18 and 19) in 2019 was 46.4%, and 88.3% for 20–24-years-old (CDC, 2021b). The birth rate increased for nonmarital births for Black mothers from 2018 to 2019, although the overall birth rate for teens and young adults has decreased over the last decade. Although reproductive health also includes infertility, maternal and child health, assisted reproductive technology (ART), and infant mortality, this chapter (and book) focuses primarily on infectious diseases (STIs and HIV), sexual violence, and sexual behavior among Black emerging adults.

Sexual Violence

Sexual violence is sexual activity and/or contact when consent is not voluntarily given. According to the CDC (2016), more than 33% of women and 25% of men have experienced sexual violence during their lifetimes. According to the campus sexual violence statistics from Rape, Abuse, & Incest National Network (RAINN, 2021), 26.4% of female undergraduate students and 6.8% of male undergraduate students experience rape or sexual assault through force, violence, or incapacitation. Due to the nature of this type of violence, it is not reported as often as other crimes, and the statistics on Black college students is limited as it has not traditionally been included in previous large-scale campus assault research. However, in 2001 the *HBCU Campus Sexual Assault* (HBCU-CSA) study was published. Data from 3,951 Black women at four different HBCUs participated in the study and results indicate 14.9% experienced an attempted or completed sexual assault before entering college, and 14.2% experienced at an attempted or completed sexual assault since entering college. Since entering college, participants reported 4.8% were assaulted through force or violence, and 3.4% occurred when the participant was incapacitated. Not much information was provided on perpetrators in this report, other than that most students who experienced a sexual assault knew the perpetrator. There is a more robust discussion on this topic in Chapter 7.

Sexual Risk Behavior

The CDC that youth between the ages of 15 and 24 make up approximately 25% of the sexually active population, yet they account for almost half (45.5%) of new STIs that occur in the United States each year (CDC, 2021a). In fact, STIs are the most reported infectious diseases in the United States. The CDC monitors eight common STIs: chlamydia, gonorrhea, trichomoniasis, human papillomavirus (HPV), herpes simplex virus (HSV), HIV, syphilis, and hepatitis B virus (HBV). Surveillance data continues to show that numbers and rates of reported chlamydia and gonorrhea cases are highest in young people between the ages of 15 and 24 (CDC (2016)). Although the media often focuses on chlamydia and gonorrhea, the two most prevalent STIs in the United States are HPV and HSV-2 (CDC (2016)). STIs threaten the sexual and reproductive health of all adolescents and young adults (Browne et al., 2009) but are especially deleterious for females. They are more vulnerable to STIs than males and may suffer more damaging consequences to their overall health and reproductive functioning. There may not be any obvious signs, as STIs can be asymptomatic, but untreated STIs can cause cancer, pelvic inflammatory disease, infertility, and other health problems for females. Younger females are more susceptible to bacterial STIs (e.g., chlamydia and gonorrhea) because of their immature cervix, and Black females who still douche are at increased risk for infections (Blythe et al., 2003). While lesbian and bisexual females may be at lower risk for certain STIs, they are still susceptible to poorer health outcomes from STIs than males. This is partially because males are more likely to notice symptoms of STIs earlier such as unusual discharge and lesions or sores (CDC (2016)) in their genital region.

HIV/AIDS

Due to the urgency of the topic of HIV/AIDS, it is important to dedicate significant space to discussing it and its impact on the Black community. STIs, including HIV are an urgent public health crisis for all Americans but particularly for Black/African Americans (CDC, 2021; Kaiser Family Foundation [KFF], 2020). Black individuals make up approximately 13% of the United States population but account for 42% of the new HIV diagnoses in 2018 (CDC, 2021). Black youth and emerging adults are disproportionately affected by HIV. The rates of HIV infection among young Black people in the 13–24 age range account for many new HIV diagnoses in the US (US Department of Health and Human Services, 2021). In fact, among Blacks in the United States, Black youth (male and female) have a disproportionately high incidence of HIV infection (KFF, 2020). The rate of new HIV diagnoses, per 100,000 among Black adolescents was eight times that of Whites, and more than twice that of Latinos. The vast majority (79%) of the diagnoses among Black men was attributed to male-to-male contact, and approximately 15% was attributed to heterosexual contact. This contrasts with Black women where the majority (92%) of new HIV diagnoses are attributed to heterosexual contact. Although HIV diagnoses among Black people decreased by 7% between 2014 and 2018 overall, there was an increase among Black people aged 25 to 34 years old. Given the extended latency period for developing observable HIV-related symptoms, it is likely that many adults with HIV were infected when they were college students (Bazargan et al., 2000), which is why studying this population is so important.

Although many of the published psychological and public health studies utilize general college populations, there needs to be more of a focus on the sexual environments of African American students, who are at an increased risk for STIs and HIV infection when compared with their nonminority peers (Bazargan et al., 2000; Grello et al., 2006). The increasing number of STI/HIV cases among Black/African Americans young adults, many who are in college, necessitates further examination of risk-related factors. Concerns that have a long history of documentation in STI/HIV related literature among college students such as inconsistent condom use (Ellis, 2016; Lewis et al., 2009; Valentine et al., 2003; Younge et al., 2018), concurrent partnerships (Lewis et al., 2009; Pittman et al., 2019), casual sex (Grello et al., 2006; Pittman et al., 2019), younger age of sexual debut (Browne et al., 2009; Hou, 2009) and alcohol and substance use in the context of sexual behavior (Gullette & Lyons, 2005; Hall & Jones, 2020) are all evident among students on HBCU campuses (Alleyne & Gaston, 2010; Lyttle et al., 2018; Murray et al., 2014; Pittman et al., 2019; Thomas et al., 2008). The CDC, in conjunction with the UNCF – Special Programs Corporation conducted a large quantitative online survey with students from HBCUs in the mid-2000s. Respondents from 24 four-year public and private HBCUs completed an assessment about HIV/AIDS knowledge and behaviors. Over 1,000 surveys were completed (51% female/76% between 18 and 21 years). Based on the survey questions, most respondents reported an average to high HIV knowledge score, perceived themselves to be low-risk, and yet reported multiple sexual partners over the past 12 months and inconsistent condom use. HBCU students take more protective measures but engage in riskier behaviors (Johnson et al., 2014). Black HBCU students also report specific protective factors at similar or higher rates than White students at predominately White institutions (PWIs) including condom use and less substance use, yet still bear a disproportionate burden of STIs/HIV (Younge et al., 2013). The next chapter focuses on the topic of identity and how its development and maintenance affect how one sees themselves, and ultimately takes care of their sexual health.

References

Alleyne, B. & Gaston, G. (2010). Gender disparity and HIV risk among young Black women in college: A literature review. *Affilia: Journal of Women and Social Work*, 25(2), 135–145.

American College Health Association. (2019). *American College Health Association-National College Health Assessment II: Reference Group Executive Summary Spring 2019*. MD: Silver Spring.

American Sexual Health Association (2021, May 26). *Understanding Sexual Health*. https://www.ashasexualhealth.org/sexual-health/

Bazargan, M., Kelly, E. M., Stein, J. A., Husaini, B. A., & Bazargan, S. H. (2000). Correlates of HIV risk-taking behaviors among African-American college students: The effect of HIV knowledge, motivation, and behavioral skills. *Journal of the National Medical Association, 92*(8), 391–404.

Blythe, M. J., Fortenberry, J. D., & Orr, D. P. (2003). Douching behaviors reported by adolescent and young adult women at high risk for sexually transmitted infections. *Journal of Pediatric and Adolescent Gynecology, 16*(2), 95–100.

Browne, D. C., Clubb, P. A., Wang, Y., & Wagner, F. (2009). Drug use and high-risk sexual behaviors among African American men who have sex with men and men who have sex with women. *American Journal of Public Health, 99*(6), 1062–1066.

Centers for Disease Control and Prevention, National Center for Injury Prevention and Control, Division of Violence Prevention. (2016). *Sexual violence: Definitions*. Retrieved from: https://www.cdc.gov/violenceprevention/sexualviolence/definitions.html

Centers for Disease Control and Prevention. (2019, June). *Sexual Health*. National Center for HIV/AIDS, Viral Hepatitis, STD, and TB Prevention. https://www.cdc.gov/sexualhealth/Default.html

Centers for Disease Control and Prevention (2021a, February). HIV and African American People. Retrieved from: https://www.cdc.gov/hiv/pdf/group/racialethnic/africanamericans/cdc-hiv-africanamericans-2021.pdf

Centers for Disease Control and Prevention (2021b, March). Births: Final Data for 2019. *National Vital Statistics Reports, 70*(2). Retrieved from: https://www.cdc.gov/nchs/data/nvsr/nvsr70/nvsr70-02-508.pdf

Ellis, E. M., Collins, R. L., Homish, G. G., Parks, K. A., & Kiviniemi, M. T. (2016). Perceived controllability of condom use shifts reliance on implicit versus explicit affect. *Health Psychology, 35*(8), 842.

Ford, J. V., Ivankovich, M. B., Douglas Jr., J. M., Hook III, E. W., Barclay, L., Elders, J., ... & Coleman, E. (2017). The need to promote sexual health in America: A new vision for public health action. *Sexually Transmitted Diseases, 44*(10), 579–585.

Grello, C. M., Welson, D. P., & Harper, M. S. (2006). No strings attached: The nature of casual sex in college students. *Journal of Sex Research, 43*, 255–267.

Gullette, D. L., & Lyons, M. A. (2005). Sexual sensation seeking, compulsivity, and HIV risk behaviors in college students. *Journal of Community Health Nursing, 22*(1), 47–60.

Hall, N. M., & Jones, J. M. (2020). Predictors of sexual risk among HBCU students: Implications for STI/HIV prevention and intervention. *Journal of Black Sexuality and Relationships, 6*(3), 71–92

Hou, S. I. (2009). HIV-related behaviors among Black students attending Historically Black Colleges and Universities (HBCUs) versus white students attending a traditionally white institution (TWI). *AIDS Care, 21*(8), 1050–1057.

Johnson, A. L., Orbe, M. P., & Cooke-Jackson, A. (2014). "Let's talk about sex": Exploring HBCU student memorable message narratives. *Howard Journal of Communications*, *25*(3), 303–323.

Kaiser Family Foundation (2020, February 7). *Black Americans and HIV/ AIDS: The Basics*. Retrieved from: https://www.kff.org/hivaids/fact-sheet/ black-americans-and-hivaids-the-basics/

Lewis, J., Miguez-Burbano, M., & Malow, R. (2009, June). HIV risk behavior among college students in the United States. *College Student Journal*, *43*, 475–491.

Lyttle, D., Montgomery, A. J., Davis, B. L., Burns, D., McGee, Z. T., & Fogel, J. (2018). An exploration using the Neuman systems model of risky sexual behaviors among African American college students: A brief report. *Journal of Cultural Diversity*, *25*(4), 142–147

Murray, A., Huang, M. J., Hardnett, F., & Sutton, M. Y. (2014). Strengthening HIV knowledge and awareness among undergraduate students at Historically Black Colleges and Universities. *Journal of Health Disparities Research and Practice*, *7*(4), 33–45.

Pittman, D. M., Kaur, P., & Eyler, L. T. (2019). Hidden in plain sight: Making a case for heterosexual Black college women being identified as a high-risk population for HIV infection. *Cultural Diversity and Ethnic Minority Psychology*, *25*(1), 104.

Rape, Abuse, & Incest National Network. (2021). Campus sexual violence: Statistics. Retrieved from: https://www.rainn.org/statistics/campus-sexual-violence

Thomas, P. E., Voetsch, A. C., Song, B., Calloway, D., Goode, C., Mundey, L...& Heffelfinger, J. D. (2008). HIV risk behaviors and testing history in historically Black college and university settings. *Public Health Reports*, *123*, 115–125.

U.S. Department of Health and Human Services (2021). *HIV National Strategic Plan for the United States: A Roadmap to End the Epidemic 2021–2025*. Washington, DC.

Valentine, P. A., Wright, D. L., & Henley, G. L. (2003). Patterns of safer sex practices among allied health students at historically Black colleges and universities. *Journal of Allied Health*, *32*, 173–178.

Younge, S.N., Corneille, M. A., Lyde, M., & Cannady, J. (2013). The paradox of risk: Historically Black college/university students and sexual health. *Journal of American College Health*, *61*(5), 254–262.

Younge, S. N., Wade, B. H., Geter, A., Holliday, R. C., & Trawick, C. (2018). Condom attitudes and condom use among first year college men attending a historically Black institution. *American Journal of Health Studies*, *33*(2), 80–88.

4   The Importance of Identity in Sexual Health

The unique identity development processes that Black individuals undergo is beyond the scope of this chapter, but it is important to introduce in hopes of more future research. Identity, identity, identity development, and identity maintenance influence the sexual health of Black college students. Often identity is only discussed in the sexual and reproductive health literature as it relates to sexual orientation; however, the lens by which young people view their choices and subsequent behaviors is guided by how they view themselves.

The importance of identity, identity development, and identity maintenance are critical topics of interest to many researchers. Identity refers to the beliefs, ideals, and values that help shape and guide a person's behavior. As Erikson (1968) noted, identity manifests itself both as an intrapersonal process of self-definition and as an interplay between the individual and important others (e.g., friends, family members). Everyone has a personal identity (*i.e.,* who am I?) and this identity is essentially one's sense of who they are. One's sense of personal identity is shaped by their experiences and interactions with others, and it is this identity that helps guide their actions, beliefs, and behaviors as they age. For some, it may take some longer than others to discover and embrace their identity, but remember, it IS a process. Having a strong personal identity is needed to establish healthy intimate relationships, which is a major goal in emerging adulthood.

The appropriateness of various behaviors and the understood or believed suitability of these practices and/or behaviors are contained within a cultural framework. Part of the cultural framework for an individual is their identity. One's identity is socially constructed and integrates historical definitions and societal interactions. An important part of this identity comes from the sense of affect held about the social group from which a person emerges or considers themselves a part. A person's sense of who they are, in a social context, is called their social identity.

DOI: 10.4324/9781003180944-4

Social identity theory (Tajfel & Turner, 1979) argues that a person's self-concept involves personal and social identity characteristics derived from an intergroup perspective. As mentioned previously, personal identity involves one's own unique aspects, personal attributes, likes, and dislikes (Emmers-Sommers & Allen, 2005). Social identity, however, involves how individuals identify themselves as members of a particular social group. This may include one's self-concept with relation to what has been considered the 'Big 8' intersectional social identities:

- **Racial identity** (e.g., Black, White) – a person's sense of group or collective identity based on one's perception that he or she shares a common heritage with a particular racial group
- **Ethnic identity** (e.g., Hispanic) – shared national, cultural, and/or linguistic heritage
- **Sexual orientation identity** (e.g., heterosexual, LGBQ, same-gender-loving)—emotional, romantic, sexual, spiritual, affections, and/or relational attraction to another person or persons
- **Gender identity** (e.g., woman, transgender man, nonbinary) – who a person sees themselves as, and it may or may not conform to the expectations of their sex at birth
- **(Dis)Ability identity** (e.g., wheelchair-bound, hearing impaired) – physical, mental, or emotional impairment that substantially limits one or more major life activities
- **Religion/Spirituality identity** (e.g., Christian, atheist) – personal or institutional systems of beliefs and practices
- **Nationality identity** (e.g., Jamaican) – a person's country of origin
- **Socioeconomic status identity** (e.g., working class, middle class) – social standing based on income and/or one's position in society

Since individuals try to create unique identities for their group and their group membership, they also try to distinguish themselves from outgroups and outgroup members. This makes topics such as sexuality, sexual orientation, casual sex, sex outside of marriage, incongruent sexual identity and behavior, and other sensitive issues related to sexual health and behavior a challenge. If the discussions surrounding promoting positive sexual health, sexuality, engaging in safer sex practices, or STIs/HIV are deemed outgroup discussions and therefore not relevant to how they see themselves, many of those conversations and practices will be avoided by students. This is seen when discussing risk perception among youth and emerging adults. Such avoidance may psychologically strengthen and/or reinforce ingroup status and membership while simultaneously increasing the risk for poor sexual health outcomes. Research demonstrates that even though young adults engage in a bevy of risky behaviors, their assessment of risk and their personalization of risk is usually less than accurate which contributes to adverse sexual health outcomes. A person's identity is intertwined with communication about sex, sexuality, and sexual health because they either support or demoralize one's identity (Rubinsky & Cooke-Johnson, 2017).

Dr. Amos Wilson, a noted Black psychologist, has a famous saying *"if we don't know who we are then we are whomever somebody tells us we are" (Wilson, 1993, p. 38)* The college environment provides a ripe setting for continued identity development through interactions with people, courses, programs, and contexts. One of the most fulfilling aspects of teaching students is when they discover something about themselves that can be integrated into their self- and sexual schemas and scripts. Sexual exploration is a normal part of the development for emerging adults, and the college environment provides the backdrop for experimentation. It should be the role of those who are guiding these young people to help them understand that much of what they are feeling, thinking, and experiencing is natural for their stage of development. There are often noticeable changes in cognition, social norms, and expectations from freshman year to graduation among individuals. Erikson (1968) believed that identity development took place in stages throughout the lifespan and has described the impact of social experience (psychosocial) and how social interaction and relationships (sociocultural) played a role in development and growth. As with most stage theories, one needs to successfully transition through one stage to go to the next. Erikson believed that at each stage there are conflicts that serve as benchmarks for development. For traditional-aged college students (18–24 years), two stages are relevant: adolescence (12 to 18) – identity vs. role confusion, and young adulthood (19–40) – intimacy vs. isolation.

- **Identity vs. Role Confusion (ages 12 to 18)**

This stage is crucial in developing a sense of personal identity which can establish the foundation for behavior and development throughout the lifespan. It is during this stage that young people explore their various roles, ideals, beliefs, and values. This can be a time of extreme confusion as adolescents may be unsure about who they are and/or insecure about who they are becoming. Their parents, guardians, mentors, and/or primary caretakers have sought to instill certain beliefs, values, and perspectives in them, and they must decide if they agree or disagree with what they have been taught. If teens are not allowed to explore these inconsistencies, they can be left in what Erikson calls *role confusion*. The consequences of role confusion are thought to result in a weaker sense of self and self-confidence, difficulties with fidelity (or commitment), and poor emotional and psychological well-being. One of the decisions that many make in this phase is whether to engage in sexual activity, which sexual behaviors to engage in, and with whom (Perkins et al., 2020)

- **Intimacy vs. Isolation (ages 19 to 40)**

Most humans have an innate desire and need to form loving relationships with other people. This stage covers the period of emerging and early adulthood when people are exploring personal relationships. The goal is to develop close, healthy, committed intimate relationships with other people. Success in this stage is posited to lead to strong relationships, while failure results in isolation. Although intimacy has been used interchangeably with sex, it is much more than sex or romance. Intimacy can be seen as a deep, reciprocal connection between individuals and is expressed in familial, friendship, and other relationships that are not sexual in nature. When one can navigate this stage of life successfully, they can develop support systems and intimate relationships with others that help to support healthy emotional and psychological well-being. The consequences of isolation can result in unhealthy or few friendships, poor relationships, and weak social support systems. These consequences may manifest in poorer psychological, physical, and/or sexual health. Hence, it is critical to understand the role that identity development plays in establishing beliefs, values, and practices about sexual health and sexual health outcomes.

As progress has been made in the identity and identity development fields, an expansion to include various aspects of identity have been pursued by researchers. Each person has various identities that can be used to describe them, but some will be more salient than others based on the socially generated norms of the society in which they live and function. At times, individuals are asked, even expected to prioritize one identity over another. Some identities are going to be more prominent in certain environments based on whether it is seen as privileged or oppressed. For example, identifying as Black at an HBCU may be seen as privileged because most students enrolled also identify that way. However, identifying as same-gender-loving may be interpreted as an oppressed identity as only a minority of students will also describe themselves that way. If a student is not secure in their sexual orientation identity (or any salient identity) it creates a situation where they will be less likely to successfully navigate the stages of development and more likely to experience the negative consequences.

A question or concern is how does one navigate multiple identities, particularly when they may be at different ends of the privileged/oppressive spectrum? Intersectionality (Crenshaw, 1989) is a framework which acknowledges that identities do not operate separately from other identities, and that the structure of power and privilege come together in interlocking, overlapping systems. Identities can be salient individually, collectively, and intersectionally. Some social identities are attached to multiple privileged groups (e.g., White heterosexual man) while others may be attached to multiple oppressed groups (e.g., Black lesbian woman), or any combination (e.g., Black heterosexual man). All these identities impact the collegiate experience and opportunities students have for growth and experience.

One of the main criticisms of identity theorists such as Erikson is the reality that people are socialized within various environments and spaces which directly, and indirectly, impact identity development (Spencer, 2008). The phenomenological variant of ecological systems theory (PVEST) is a developmental theory that situates identity formation within context and emphasizes socialization and how individuals make 'sense' of experiences (Velez & Spencer, 2018). Velez and Spencer posit that key insights from intersectionality, such as the emphasis on multiple sources of privilege and powers, are complementary with PVEST. Black youth and emerging adults in the United States undergo the normative developmental routes; however, the added experience of racial prejudice and discrimination, and its history of pathologizing Black sexuality may manifest in a different identity maturation process. PVEST is important in discussing identity and development among Black college students because how individuals cope with their context is instrumental in their establishment of identity, which allows adaptive functioning (Brittian, 2012). This is one of the reasons why HBCUs and their context are so important for students. Concepts such as racial pride and uplift and leadership development are foundational to HBCUs and are crucial for the development of a sound, healthy identity.

More research needs to be done on the influence of the college environment on how identity is formed, molded, and communicated by Black HBCU students. The ability to 'read' the environment is important – what are the norms? what is acceptable? what is not acceptable? who is important? The next section provides additional insight into racial and ethnic identity development.

Racial and Ethnic Identity

Overwhelmingly, most of the identity work with Black emerging adults has been investigating their racial and ethnic identity. Racial identity theories can be contrasted with conceptualizations of identity among other important personal attributes. Other personal attributes may be salient, but the key defining feature of one's social group for many Black people appears to be race (Sellers et al., 1997). There is a difference in opinion regarding appropriate terminology for describing the social identity for Black individuals. Some scholars prefer the term *ethnic identity* because of the lack of clarity regarding what constitutes a 'race.' Ethnic identity often is viewed as an individual's identification with

> *a segment of a larger society whose members are thought, by themselves or others, to have a common origin and share segments of a common culture and who, in addition, participate in shared activities in which the common origin and culture are significant ingredients.* (Yinger, 1976, p. 200)

Essentially, ethnic identity explores the individual within the larger society.

Several studies with Black college students have found that stronger ethnic identity is associated with less risky drug use (Bowman Heads et al., 2018; Corneille & Belgrave, 2007) and sexual attitudes (Belgrave et al., 2000), higher sexual refusal efficacy (Corneille & Belgrave, 2007; Salazar et al., 2004), less risky sexual behavior (Beadnell et al., 2003; Hall & Jones, 2020), and less alcohol and marijuana use (Pugh & Bry, 2007). Higher ethnic identity is thought to serve as a component of healthy identity development for young Black individuals that may protect them from pressure to engage in risky sexual behavior and drug use (Townsend et al., 2010). However, more recent studies with Black college students at HBCUs demonstrate mixed results in the relevance of ethnic identity in sexual decision-making and sexual health outcomes. Corneille et al. (2012) investigated ethnic identity, along with masculinity ideology, as predictors of healthy relationships and engagement in sexually protective methods. A sample of 92 sexually active young, self-identified heterosexual Black men attending an HBCU in the mid-Atlantic region of the United States participated in a quantitative survey. The researchers hypothesized that stronger ethnic identity would be associated with higher relationship mutuality and increased sexually protective behaviors, measured by condom use and number of sexual partners in the past 3 months. Results indicated that those with higher ethnic identity did evidence greater intimate relationship mutuality, but it was not significantly related to condom use or number of partners.

Heads et al. (2017) and Hall and Jones (2020) found similar results when examining ethnic identity in relation to risky sexual behavior and substance use among Black college students attending HBCUs. Heads et al. reported results from 237 Black HBCU students (2/3 of sample identified as female) which indicated that ethnic identity was related to fewer incidents of engaging in heavy drinking and unprotected sexual intercourse; however, these relationships were not statistically significant. Hall and Jones described findings from 351 Black undergraduate students (43.3% male/ 81.5% heterosexual) which showed that ethnic identity was related to sexual behavior and substance use but was not a significant predictor of any of the sexual behavior variables and/or HIV risk behaviors.

Other scholars, including the author, prefer the term *racial identity* because race, at least in the United States, it is often described as the single most important aspect of a Black person's social identity (Helms, 1990) and it is based *"on a sense of group or collective identity based on one's perception that he or she shares a common heritage with a particular racial group"* (Helms, 1993, p. 3). Because of racial segregation in the United States, and the unique historical experiences, the majority of Black Americans compare themselves not with members of the broader society but other Black Americans (Rowley et al., 1998; Sellers et al., 1998).

Since its infancy, racial identity researchers have grappled with the significance and meaning of the construct. Racial identity development has been theorized to take place through stages of development such as the Nigrescence model (Cross, 1991) or to be multidimensional in nature such as posited by the multidimensional model of racial identity (MMRI, Sellers et al., 1997). In previous research, Rowley et al. (1998) examined the relationship between racial identity, self-esteem, and health risk behaviors. Their results showed that higher levels of centrality (a dimension of racial identity) were positively related to self-esteem and less health risk and risk-taking behaviors. Researchers speculated that if sexual behaviors are like other types of health risk behaviors, it is likely that greater racial centrality is associated with decreased sexual risk-taking.

Walker et al. (2015) conducted a study examining racial and sexual identity, and sexual risk behavior among young Black gay and bisexual men. Researchers used the MMRI (Sellers et al., 1998) to measure racial identity and then modified it to focus on sexual identity. Participants were asked to indicate how important each identity was to them, and to also indicate how many times they engaged in eight sexual behaviors (protected and unprotected by a condom). More than half (55%) of the sample identified as college students. Findings indicated that students with higher levels of racial identity, measured by racial centrality and public regard, reported fewer unprotected sexual acts and encounters. Although racial identity was related to sexual behavior, sexual identity was not.

Based on the published work that has been conducted on HBCU campuses, more research needs to be done to examine the relationship between racial and/or ethnic identity and decisions about sexual health and sexual risk behaviors. Much of the identity literature for Black students speaks to racial identity development, but more needs to focus on intersection of race and gender and its relationship to sexual health and behaviors. How are they connected, and how can they be enhanced for prevention efforts? An important first step that is important to undertake is identifying whether racial and/or ethnic identity is conceptualized by current students in the same ways in which the instruments conceptualized them when they were developed. Based on observations of, and conversations with currently enrolled Black traditional college-aged students, their conceptualization of identity related to race and how to define 'Blackness' are layered. As mentioned in the *Introduction*, the cultural shifts and swings of the student population must be taken into consideration. Students are coming in with views on race and identity that are foundationally different than the previous generation (Millennials) of students, whose are perhaps different from the generation before them (Generation X). Along with understanding and exploring their racial identity, students are understanding how their racial and gender identities intersect to influence their perspectives and experiences.

Gendered Racial Identity

Identity is important to minoritized, marginalized, and oppressed groups (Zamani-Gallaher, 2017). Traditionally, gender has been defined and limited in research to binary categories that are heavily associated with biological sex (Jones et al., 2018). There are students, staff, and faculty who do not ascribe to the gender binary, nor do they desire to be associated with the roles that society deems are appropriate for a particular gender. Gender identity is one's conceptualization of themselves, which is not always in line with their biological sex, or the sex assigned to them at birth. Much of the work on intersectional identities has been done with Black women and less is known about the intersectional nature of Black men and individuals who do not identify with the gender binary, and their sexual health outcomes. The literature on Black sexual minorities (i.e., LGTBQ+) in college, and at HBCUs have grown over the past decade

(Patton et al., 2020), but more is needed especially as it relates to identity and sexual health. Squire and Mobley (2015) investigated college choice based on the salience of race and sexuality among 10 Black sexual minority men. Results indicated that men who identified more with their Black identity often chose to attend an HBCU, while those who identified more with their sexual identity enrolled at a PWI. This is interesting because many HBCUs are believed, by some, to be homophobic spaces and that those who identify as sexual minorities are sure to endure additional stress on campus. Given the importance of both racial and sexual identity for young Black gay and bisexual men, it is important to investigate the conflations. Often, 'gayness' is conflated with Whiteness or being a race-traitor, and 'Blackness' is often conflated with heterosexuality and hyper-masculine performances (Lenning, 2017).

Race and gender are often separated in the literature and associated with health outcomes separately; however, seminal work in psychology and public health (Cole, 2009) show us that multiple identities influence the self for Black men and women. Gendered racial identity is the intersection of racial identity and gender identity (Thomas et al., 2011, 2013). Based on the unique history of Black people in the United States, it is difficult for many to separate the two identities.

Research shows that the influence of racial and gender socialization messages affects the development of their gendered racial identity. For instance, the media images and societal stereotypes of Black women as oversexualized shape the perception of Black women and girls' sexuality and the ways they view and identify themselves (Stephens & Phillips, 2003; Townsend et al., 2010; Williams & Lewis, 2021). While there is not much published work on the relationship between gendered racial identity and sexual health and behavior, Leath et al. (2022) found that participants in their qualitative study who felt more positive about intersectional identity as a Black woman reported greater sexual assertiveness and satisfaction (Leath et al., 2022).

Much of the research on gendered racial identity has also been conducted with Black women because of their double minority status ('Black' and 'woman'). However, on most college campuses Black men, with the rare exception, are considered the minority in the 'community.' While Black men experience racism and sexism in a different manner than Black women, it is important to not minimize either experiences. These experiences inform their development, and through socialization, their attitudes and views on sexual health and behaviors. Racial socialization is how parents, guardians, and caretakers teach children about race. Often these messages are gendered and include the expectations for how Black men and women conduct themselves interpersonally. What is missing in the literature is not only more investigation into how Black men see the intersection of race and gender, but how do Black individuals who do not identify with the gender binary reconcile this? This question, and many others, are explored in subsequent chapters which investigate various psychosocial, sociocultural, and contextual factors critical among Black college students within the milieu of HBCUs, and how this environment can promote positive, and inclusive, sexual health for its students.

References

Beadnell, B., Stielstra, S., Baker, S., Morrison, D. M., Knox, K., Gutierrez, L., & Doyle, A. (2003). Ethnic identity and sexual risk-taking among African-American women enrolled in an HIV/STD prevention intervention. *Psychology, Health & Medicine, 8*(2), 187–198.

Belgrave, F. Z., Van Oss Marin, B., & Chambers, D. B. (2000). Cultural, contextual, and intrapersonal predictors of risky sexual attitudes among urban African American girls in early adolescence. *Cultural Diversity and Ethnic Minority Psychology, 6*(3), 309.

Brittian, A. S. (2012). Understanding African American adolescents' identity development: A relational developmental systems perspective. *Journal of Black Psychology, 38*(2), 172–200.

Bowman Heads, A. M., Glover, A. M., Castillo, L. G., Blozis, S., & Kim, S. Y. (2018). Dimensions of ethnic identity as protective factors for substance use and sexual risk behaviors in African American college students. *Journal of American College Health, 66*(3), 178–186.

Cole, E. R. (2009). Intersectionality and research in psychology. *American Psychologist, 64*(3), 170.

Corneille, M. A., & Belgrave, F. Z. (2007). Ethnic identity, neighborhood risk, and adolescent drug and sex attitudes and refusal efficacy: The urban African American girls' experience. *Journal of Drug Education, 37*(2), 177–190.

Corneille, M., Fife, J. E., Belgrave, F. Z., & Sims, B. C. (2012). Ethnic identity, masculinity, and healthy sexual relationships among African American men. *Psychology of Men & Masculinity, 13*(4), 393–399. 10.1037/a0026878

Crenshaw, K. (1989). Demarginalizing the intersection of race and sex: A Black feminist critique of antidiscrimination doctrine, feminist theory and antiracist politics. *University of Chicago Legal Forum, 1989*, 139–167.

Cross, W. E. (1991). *Shades of Black: Diversity in African-American identity.* Philadelphia: Temple University Press.

Emmers-Sommers, T. M., & Allen, M. (2005). *Safer sex in personal relationships: The role of sexual scripts in HIV infection and prevention.* Mahwah, NJ: Lawrence Erlbaum Associates.

Erikson, E. H. (1968). *Identity: Youth in crisis.* New Yor: W. W. Norton.

Hall, N.M., & Jones, J. M. (2020). Predictors of sexual risk among HBCU students: Implications for STI/HIV prevention and intervention. *Journal of Black Sexuality and Relationships, 6*(3), 71–92

Heads, A. M., Dickson, J. W., & Asby, A. T. (2017). Correlates of HIV risk-taking behaviors among African-American college students: HIV knowledge and ethnic identity. *Journal of Health Care for the Poor and Underserved, 28*(2), 155–170.

Helms, J. E. (1990). *Black and White racial identity: Theory, research, and practice.* Greenwood Press.

Helms, J. E. (1993). I also said, "White racial identity influences White researchers." *The Counseling Psychologist, 21*(2), 240–243.

Jones, M. K., Buque, M., & Miville, M. L. (2018). African American gender roles: A content analysis of empirical research from 1981 to 2017. *Journal of Black Psychology, 44*(5), 450–486. 10.1177/0095798418783561

Leath, S., Jones, M., Jerald, M. C., & Perkins, T. R. (2022). An investigation of Jezebel stereotype awareness, gendered racial identity and sexual beliefs and behaviours among Black adult women. *Culture, Health & Sexuality, 24*(4), 517–532.

Lenning, E. (2017). Unapologetically queer in unapologetically Black spaces: Creating an inclusive HBCU campus. *Humboldt Journal of Social Relations, 39*, 283–293.

Patton, L. D., Blockett, R. A., & McGowan, B. L. (2020). Complexities and contradictions: Black lesbian, gay, bisexual, and queer students' lived realities across three urban HBCU contexts. Urban Education, 1–28.

Perkins, E. L., Chacon, F., Obizoba, C., Stennis, K. B., Wutoh, R., Madison, L., Wells, G., & Turner, D. (2020). Determinants of risky sexual behaviors in an HBCU community. *Journal of Mental Health and Social Behaviour, 2*(1), 116. 10.33790/jmhsb1100116.

Pugh, L. A., & Bry, B. H. (2007). The protective effects of ethnic identity for alcohol and marijuana use among Black young adults. *Cultural Diversity and Ethnic Minority Psychology, 13*(2), 187.

Rowley, S. J., Sellers, R. M., Chavous, T. M., & Smith, M.A. (1998). The relationship between racial identity and self-esteem in African American college and high school students. *Journal of Personality and Social Psychology, 74*, 715–724.

Rubinsky, V., & Cooke-Johnson, A. (2017). "Tell me something other than to use a condom and sex is scary": Memorable messages whom and gender minorities wish for and recall about sexual health. *Women's Studies in Communication, 40*(4), 379–400.

Salazar, L. F., DiClemente, R. J., Wingood, G. M., Crosby, R. A., Harrington, K., Davies, S., & Oh, M. K. (2004). Self-concept and adolescents' refusal of unprotected sex: A test of mediating mechanisms among African American girls. *Prevention Science, 5*(3), 137–149.

Sellers, R. M., Rowley, S. A. J., Chavous, T. M., Shelton, J. N., & Smith, M. A. (1997). Multidimensional inventory of Black identity: A preliminary investigation of reliability and construct validity. *Journal of Personality and Social Psychology, 73*(4), 805–815. 10.1037/0022-3514.73.4.805

Sellers, R. M., Smith, M. A., Shelton, J. N., Rowley, S. A., & Chavous, T. M. (1998). Multidimensional model of racial identity: A reconceptualization of African American racial identity. *Personality and Social Psychology Review, 2*(1), 18–39.

Spencer, M. B. (2008). Phenomenology and ecological systems theory: Development of diverse groups. In W. Damon & R. M. Lerner (Eds.), Child and adolescent development: An advanced course , (pp. 696–735). New York: Wiley Publishers.

Squire, D. D., & Mobley, S. D. (2015). Negotiating race and sexual orientation in the college choice process of Black gay males. *The Urban Review, 47*(3), 466–491.

Stephens, D. P., & Phillips, L. D. (2003). Freaks, gold diggers, divas, and dykes: The sociohistorical development of adolescent African American women's sexual scripts. *Sexuality and Culture, 7*(1), 3–49.

Tajfel, H., & Turner, J. C. (1979). An integrative theory of intergroup conflict. In W. C. Austin & S. Worchel (Eds.), *The social psychology of intergroup relations* (pp. 33–53). Monterey, CA: Brooks/Cole.

Thomas, A. J., Hacker, J. D., & Hoxha, D. (2011). Gendered racial identity of Black young women. *Sex Roles: A Journal of Research, 64*(7–8), 530–542. 10.1007/s11199-011-9939-y

Thomas, A. J., Hoxha, D., & Hacker, J. D. (2013). Contextual influences on gendered racial identity development of African American young women. *Journal of Black Psychology, 39*(1), 88–101.

Townsend, T. G., Thomas, A. J., Neilands, T. B., & Jackson, T. R. (2010). I'm no Jezebel; I am young, gifted, and Black: Identity, sexuality, and Black girls. *Psychology of Women Quarterly, 34*(3), 273–285. 10.1111/j.1471-6402. 2010.01574.x.

Velez, G., & Spencer, M. B. (2018). Phenomenology and intersectionality: Using PVEST as a frame for adolescent identity formation amid intersecting ecological systems of inequality. In C. E. Santos & R. B. Toomey (Eds.), *Envisioning the Integration of an Intersectional Lens in Developmental Science. New Directions for Child and Adolescent Development, 161,* 75–90.

Walker, J. N. J., Longmire-Avital, B., & Golub, S. (2015). Racial and sexual identities as potential buffers to risky sexual behavior for Black gay and bisexual emerging adult men. *Health Psychology, 34*(8), 841.

Williams, M. G., & Lewis, J. A. (2021). Developing a conceptual framework of Black women's gendered racial identity development. *Psychology of Women Quarterly, 45*(2), 212–228.

Wilson, A. N. (1993). *The falsification of Afrikan consciousness: Eurocentric history, psychiatry, and the politics of white supremacy.* Afrikan World InfoSystems.

Yinger, J. M. (1976). Ethnicity in complex societies. In L. A. Coser and O. N. Larsen (Eds.), *The uses of controversy in sociology.* New York: Free Press.

Zamani-Gallaher, E. M. (2017). Conflating gender and identity: The need for gender-fluid programming in community colleges. *New Directions for Community Colleges, 2017*(179), 89–99.

5 Psychosocial Influences on Sexual Health

Psychosocial influences are those variables related to an individual's psychological state and/or social environment and contribute to sexual health decisions and outcomes. The importance of investigating these variables to design more effective prevention and intervention programs for young Black college students is crucial. While there are a plethora of psychosocial factors influencing the sexual health of young Black college students, this chapter focuses on five that are documented in the literature.

Condom Attitudes and Use

Research indicates important factors in whether individuals use condoms are their attitudes and perceptions of condoms (Browne et al., 2009; Elifson et al., 2010). Inconsistent condom use is related to increased risk for poor sexual and reproductive health outcomes such as unplanned pregnancies and STIs, including HIV (Leivo et al., 2021). Although the results of studies examining condom attitudes and use among Black college students are mixed, many indicate that Black students report more consistent condom use than their White collegiate counterparts (see Hall et al., 2014). Although Black students report greater condom use in studies, they still report disproportionate STI rates. Recent research done by Younge et al. (2018) found that among 1,117 first-year Black male HBCU students, those holding positive views toward condoms were significantly more likely to have used them in their last sexual encounter. Perkins et al. (2020) conducted a study with 364 Black college students (61.3% female) attending an HBCU. The study tested hypotheses regarding gender differences in HIV/AIDS knowledge, condom attitudes and use, and frequency of sexual risk behaviors. Females were hypothesized to have better condom attitudes and use than males. There was a significant

DOI: 10.4324/9781003180944-5

difference in condom attitudes and use, such that females had more positive attitudes than men; however, more than half of the respondents (males and females) reported not using condoms at all. Additionally, juniors and seniors (upperclassman) reported using condoms less than the freshman and sophomore students. For females in this study, positive attitudes toward condom use did not result in increased safer sex behaviors.

In a more recent study, Hall, and Jones (2020) assessed condom attitudes and use among 351 Black HBCU (43% male, 87.5% heterosexual) students, aged 18–24 years. Results indicated more positive condom attitudes were associated with greater likelihood of use for oral, vaginal, and anal sex. Additional findings included males having more negative condom attitudes than females, students who self-identified as heterosexual had more negative attitudes toward condoms than LGBTQ+ students, and more negative condom attitudes from males were significantly related to risker sexual behavior such as engaging in sexual activity with strangers. In reviewing the literature on the attitudes toward, and perceptions of condoms among Black college students, four significant influences are frequently discussed.

Perceived Risk

One of the documented challenges with sexual health prevention and intervention with emerging adults is the often-distorted perception of risk based on real or assumed factors. Some individuals believe they can look at a person and accurately access their risk, or if someone meets a certain criterion (e.g., 'he looks clean,' 'she is a church girl') they are believed to be at lower risk. Additionally, they may underestimate their actual risk for infection and transmission. Previous findings suggest the decision to not use a condom in spontaneous sexual encounters is related to the perception of risk of the partner (Browne et al., 2009; Elifson et al., 2010), and feeling as if they are not *really* at risk for serious consequences (Adefuye et al., 2009; El Bcheraoui et al., 2013). Overall, the misperception of risk is a theme seen throughout the sexual health literature with emerging adults.

Relationship Status

The decision to use condoms is often based on the perceived relationship status with the partner(s). The status is often based upon either the type of relationship, or the amount of time the individuals have known each other. For example, McLaurin-Jones et al. (2017)

conducted a qualitative study with 100 Black women (ages 18–24) and had an open dialogue about condom use. There was low condom use in monogamous relationship, and an increase in condom use when one partner suspected discord, such as infidelity, in the relationship. Participants did not stop engaging in sexual activity with the partner(s) suspected of infidelity, but they used protective measures more frequently. Using data from the *Online College Social Life Survey* (8.1% Black), Hall et al. (2019) found that students who were unsure of their relationship status or intentions, and those who did not want a relationship with their partner(s) were more likely to use condoms during vaginal sex. Coleman et al. (2018) conducted six focus groups (N = 36) with Black men attending an HBCU investigating what factors facilitate condom use. The students noted that time in the relationship was a major factor in condom use with a partner. Like the McLaurin-Jones study, participants noted that the relationship may begin with condom use but eventually condoms are no longer used, based on time and/or emotional attachment to the partner(s). With emerging adults, much of the literature talks about the trend of delaying long-term monogamous relationships in favor of shorter-term casual ones. For instance, Chandler et al. (2021) found that some of the Black women in the study investigating their sexual health concerns on HBCU campuses were engaging in serial monogamy (a succession of monogamous relationships) and were demonstrating inconsistent and decreased condom use in these relationships. Oftentimes, because of the size of the HBCU campuses individuals are having sex within a small network, which increases the risk of acquiring and transmitting STIs.

Stigma

Even though there has been numerous social marketing and public health campaigns over the past two decades focused on increasing condom use, there is still a stigma associated with condom use among many subpopulations. Norwood and Zhang (2015) sampled 424 African American women college students and found that participants who were concerned with embarrassment while purchasing a condom held unfavorable attitudes toward using condoms. Negative attitudes toward condoms often translate into less frequent condom use. Johnson (2017) conducted a metanalysis of studies exploring sexual behaviors of HBCU students published between 2000 and 2016 and found that embarrassment about buying and discussing condoms was still identified as a barrier by students. Much of the stigma expressed by students appears to be attached to women who readily have condoms available or insist on using condoms in sexual interactions. Anecdotally, students have remarked "what are you carrying condoms for...do you have something?" For those young people who may not have a strong personal or sexual agency, may feel the need to 'prove' that they do not have 'something' and agree to engage in sexual activity without a barrier method.

Poor Negotiation and Communication Skills

It is daunting to be expected to have good negotiation skills, particularly for youth and emerging adults. A sample of 43 heterosexually active African American males felt it was difficult to communicate their sexual history, their sexual satisfaction, and to discuss condom use with their partners. These difficulties lead to challenges in finding intimacy and practicing safer sex and using condoms regularly (Graham, et al., 2016). Stokes and Brody (2019) investigated self-silencing among 57 Black college-aged women and its relationship to condom use frequency. Self-silencing is the tendency to inhibit one's self-expression to avoid conflict and the possibility of the loss of the relationship (Jack, 1991) Participants who displayed higher levels of self-silencing showed significant decreased odds of condom use frequency.

While there are male and female condoms, the use of female condoms as a protective barrier is relatively low among young people and not discussed in detail here. Some of the advantages of female condoms are that they are less likely than male condoms to break or tear, it is larger and can cover more area to prevent more infections, it is not made of latex (for those who have latex sensitivity or allergies) and can be inserted prior to sexual activity to not interrupt spontaneity. The disadvantages include cost (they are more expensive), they are not thought to be as effective as male condoms in preventing STIs, including HIV, and there is only one FDA-approved brand in the United States (Yarber & Sayad, 2018). Despite these problems, the female condom is an option that should be considered when discussing sexual activity and protective barrier methods with college students.

Religiosity and Spirituality

Given that many HBCUs were founded with strong ties to religious organizations, an important characteristic to explore in this population is religiosity and its relationship to sexual health (Thompson-Robinson et al., 2005; Younge et al., 2013). Generally, the term 'religiosity' denotes attendance, beliefs, practices, and behaviors associated with religious organizations (Miller & Thoreson, 2003). It is associated with doctrines, rituals, and organized worship. Spirituality is described as more of a relational phenomenon and related to the internalization and expression of positive values (Mattis, 2000). Both religion and spirituality are deeply rooted in traditional Black American culture and were thought to be vital in survival during slavery (Mbiti, 1990) and an important coping mechanism for navigating through the current times (Kogan et al., 2008).

There have been mixed results on the relationship between religiosity and sexual behavior with Black youth and emerging adults. However, in most studies that include diverse gender representation, Black women significantly identified as being more religious than men (Hall & Jones, 2020; Poulson, et al. 2008; Thompson-Robinson et al., 2005). In a study with 186 African American young people (18–21 years), Kogan et al. (2008) found that high religiosity attenuated the impact of substance use on sexual risk behavior. Students who believed themselves to be more religious used substances less and engaged in fewer sexual risk behaviors, namely consistent condom use. Around the same time, Washington et al. (2009) surveyed a group of sexually active Black males at an HBCU and found a similar result. Students who reported religion was an important element in their lives were more likely to use condoms than those students for whom religion was not seen as important. For these students, religion (or religiosity) acted as a buffer for risky sexual behavior. The reasons behind this relationship are not entirely clear. One possibility is that for those whom religion is more important may place a higher value on prevention and protection. Another possibility, although more cynical, is that condoms are just a mechanism to prevent pregnancy and STIs/HIV which, if acquired, would be a clear indication of being sexually active while also being unmarried. There is conflicting information about the relationship between religiosity and sexual risk-taking behaviors suggesting that additional empirical research is needed to understand this relationship more fully within the HBCU community.

Thomas and Freeman (2011) conducted a descriptive study with 100 Black women at an HBCU to assess whether religiosity was an influential factor in sexual risk-taking behaviors, or if the behaviors differed by levels of religiosity. Results indicated that religiosity was not a significant factor in students sexual decision-making or subsequent sexual risk-taking behavior. In unpublished research with HBCU students by the author, Black women who identified as more religious engaged in *more* sexual risk behavior than those who identified as either 'not religious at all' or 'not very religious.' More in-depth study on this relationship is warranted as the positive relationship between religion and sexual risk behavior seems counterintuitive; however, two possible explanations, or mediating factors, are suggested for young Black women. The desire for intimacy and/or a relationship, which was briefly discussed in the condom attitudes and use section, trumps the decision to engaged in protective behaviors. Additionally, the influence of the gender role imbalance on relationship formation and maintenance may play a role in sexual risk-taking by heterosexual women in college. This is discussed more in Chapter 6, *Sociocultural Influences on Sexual Health*.

The relationship between religiosity and sexual risk behaviors has been explored in research; however, the concept of spirituality and its relationship to sexual risk is less investigated. Spirituality, and religiosity, can be important resources for dealing with one's emotional and psychological distress, but they have often been used interchangeably in research. Mattis (2000) suggests that the constructs are different, and that religiosity and religious practices may serve as a vehicle through which spirituality is achieved. In a recent study, Boyd-Starke et al. (2011) investigated how dimensions of religiosity *and* spirituality influenced sexual risk behavior among 256 Black students (22.3% males) at two HBCUs. Researchers used the *Expressions of Spirituality Inventory* (MacDonald, 2000) which identifies five dimensions: cognitive orientation toward spirituality, experiential/phenomenological dimensions of spirituality, existential well-being, paranormal beliefs, and religiousness. Results confirmed the relationship between religiosity and spirituality and sexual risk behavior, but only on certain dimensions. The cognitive orientation toward spirituality (measures spiritual beliefs, attitudes, and perceptions pertaining to everyday experiences) and existential well-being (spirituality reflected in the sense of meaning and purpose in life and the ability to cope with life's uncertainties) subscales were significantly related to less sexual risk behavior. Interestingly, religiousness (includes religious practices such as attendance or affiliation) was not a significant predictor of risky sexual behavior. These results indicated that students may be more oriented toward a belief system that governs their lives and not necessarily a doctrine that has certain practices or activities.

Although HBCUs are overwhelmingly associated with Christianity, it is not the only religion to which Black students subscribe. Along those same lines, Black churches are not monolithic and there are several different religious denominations and beliefs that distinguish people from each other. If we focus on Christianity which has numerous denominations, or even Islam, the teachings are often around abstinence until marriage. If most Black traditional-aged college students are not married, a fundamental question to explore is whether young people are ascribing to these beliefs any longer?

Overall, more work needs to be done for many reasons but particularly because religion and spirituality and understood and enacted differently by young people. As a faculty member who often talks about the connection between religion, spirituality, and health, students often do not see some of the principles in religious doctrine as transferrable to modern times. This section is not to argue whether this is accurate, but to present an opportunity for the development of culturally responsive approaches to researching the topic and working with our students. It is not what the researcher believes that is important but what the participants believe and practice. In working with emerging adults, a phrase that is often repeated is *"I'm not religious, I'm more spiritual."* The question that must be grappled with is what does this mean and how can this help us to improve the sexual health of the students? If spirituality and the belief in something greater than oneself are significant, how can this be integrated into programming, prevention, and intervention efforts? If one identifies as more religious and adherence to a certain doctrine and regular attendance is what is important, what is it that they believe? How is it related to health and well-being? The work from Boyd-Starke investigated multiple dimensions of religion and spirituality and found that students can endorse some, but not all dimensions of it. Which dimensions are more heavily endorsed by the students, and what is its connection to sexual health? For example, working with students who support more 'traditional' beliefs and views on gender roles, one may focus on how to pick a partner who is supportive of these beliefs, and not admonishing the student for their beliefs. How do we utilize the strengths of HBCUs and what they stand for to truly understand the relationship with sexual health? For instance, the Afrocentric value of collectivism may be a way to start a conversation about sexual health (and other types of health) by connecting self-care as a way of honoring the communities, ancestors, and higher power(s). In sum, how do researchers, administrators, and facilitators move away from the need to be right and focus on the need to be healthy?

Mental Health

As a psychologist, the amount of attention given to the mental health of young people by educational institutions is not sufficient to facilitate optimal well-being. Most faculty and staff at institutions of higher education in the United States would probably agree that the influx of students with diagnosed and undiagnosed, treated, and untreated, mental health concerns has increased over the past decade. With more students presenting with acute, and chronic, mental health needs, it is imperative that universities offer more culturally relevant and culturally responsive programs and services for them. The transition to college from high school is discussed elsewhere in this book; however, it is important to keep reiterating how stressful, yet important these rites of passage can be for young people. In fact, many HBCUs have a rites-of-passage-type ceremony for incoming students so that they can absorb the magnitude of this new stage of life. For example, Winston-Salem State University (WSSU), a public HBCU in North Carolina has a 'Through the Archway' ceremony during Ramdition (the equivalent of freshman orientation week). The ceremony is an "opportunity to celebrate the huge step that our newest students are taking in their lives, both into adulthood and into a new and exciting collegiate experience" (WSSU, 2021).

While beginning a collegiate career is exciting, it is also a vulnerable time for students due to the physical and psychological stress that results from leaving a familiar environment and moving into a new one (Williams et al., 2021). Many students are leaving their friends and family support networks and moving to a location where they do not know anyone, and the student will need to re-introduce, and sometimes re-invent themselves. During this time, some students experience a decline in healthy eating habits, physical activity, and even engaging in preventative care. This new environment may lead to self-doubt, questioning oneself and abilities, and engaging in negative or maladaptive coping behaviors such as self-medicating and/or soothing, alcohol and substance use, and increased sexual activity (Crepaz & Marks, 2001).

Overall, research on the mental health of Black college students remain an understudied area (Lipson et al., 2018), but the relationship between mental health and sexual health of students is almost non-existent in the literature. One can argue that the exception in the literature is with Black college students who identify as LGBTQ+ (i.e., sexual minorities), but even so, the amount of data and findings is not sufficient compared to the robust body of work on White students. When focusing on Black emerging adults in college, the two predominant mental health conditions studied, irrespective of gender or sexual identity, are anxiety and depression. It is important to explore these two conditions as poor reproductive and sexual health, and sexual risk-taking behaviors have been associated with symptoms of anxiety and depression (Alvy et al., 2011; Jackson, et al., 2015; Khan et al., 2009; Lehrer et al. 2006).

Anxiety is the feeling of uneasiness and apprehension that disrupts the normal psychological state of an individual (Johnson, 2006). Students feel anxious about courses, professors, tests, relationships, finances, etc. High anxiety is often related to seeking acceptance from others and/or living with chronic fear of rejection (Giordano et al., 2017). These traits can put students in positions where they are unable to negotiate safer sex practices and may engage in negative (or harmful) behaviors to maintain relationships. The literature examining anxiety among Black college students is limited as most studies either focus on adults and/or youth. One of the few studies found included young Black individuals, but not necessarily college students. Turner et al. (2011) examined the relationship between anxiety and sexual behavior among a sample of 617 participants and found that those with elevated levels of anxiety were significantly less likely to use condoms. While these results may seem counterintuitive, anxiety is related to avoidance coping strategies (McKirnan et al., 1996). Therefore, those with increased anxiety may avoid the social interaction needed to negotiate condom use with partners.

Depression, persistent feelings of sadness and loss of interest, has been found to be associated with increased sexual risk (Alvy et al., 2011). Studies with Black youth and young adults found that depressive symptoms were associated with higher numbers of sexual partners (Turner et al., 2011), sexual sensation-seeking, unprotected sex, the prevalence of STIs, and inconsistent condom use (Jackson et al., 2015). Much of the data we have on the relationship between depression (or depressive symptomatology) is with Black college women, not men. A meta-analysis of sexual risk reduction interventions designed for Black women found that studies whose outcomes showed a significant reduction in depressive symptoms for participants also demonstrated reduced sexual risk behaviors (see Lennon et al., 2012). Recently, Hall and Jones (2020) conducted a study with both Black college men and women and found that increased depressive symptomatology was significantly related to decreased likelihood of HIV testing among 351 Black HBCU college students. Regular HIV testing is recommended for all sexually active individuals. While there are numerous factors that can be related to the decision for a young person to not get tested for HIV, it is also possible that depressive symptomology is related to a lack of sexual self-care and preventative methods for individuals.

The literature reveals that increased anxiety and depression may be related to sexual risk behavior both directly and indirectly through other variables and mechanisms, such as microaggressions (Marks and Çiftçi, 2019). Mental health is often seen as an outcome variable in research studies; however, more recent published research shows the mediating and moderating influence it has on sexual health outcomes. Jerald et al. (2017) demonstrated that when young Black women in college internalize negative stereotypes about their identities (e.g., racial, gender, sexuality), they are at risk for more mental health concerns, more substance use, negative sexual views, and riskier sexual behaviors. Leivo et al. (2021) noted that negative affect (from a variety of sources) can contribute to the development of depressive or anxious symptomatology, which is correlated with riskier sexual behavior and poorer sexual health outcomes. Avery et al., (2021) surveyed 640 Black college women about ways their appearance may influence their sexual attitudes and behaviors. Results reveal that endorsement of hegemonic ideals of beauty was linked to more negative sexual emotions such as guilt and shame. Hegemonic ideals of beauty support the belief that Eurocentric aesthetics, such as thinner noses and bodies are more feminine and more attractive than those features associated with an African esthetic (e.g., wider noses, full lips, larger bodies). One of the long-standing ideals of beauty in the Black community is related to skin tone. Colorism, which is prejudice or discrimination based on skin tone (Hall et al., 2020) may play a role in sexual risk behavior among young Black college students. Crooks et al. (2020) conducted a qualitative study with 20 Black participants about how the intersection of race, gender, age, education, and sexuality influences sexual health risk. Participants in the study identified colorism as an influence in sexual risk behavior by describing how Black women feel pressure to live up to social standards of beauty that are often based on White women and White standards. Not being able to meet those standards, or those projected in the media, perpetuates a cycle of internalized oppression and negative affect that can result in poor sexual decision-making to self-soothe.

An obvious major gap in the literature surrounding mental health needs of Black college students is a lack of focus on Black men. The available empirical studies documenting the mental health needs and challenges of young Black men in college are appalling. Particularly because those studies that are available show they are at increased risk of developing anxiety and depression (Mouzon et al., 2016) due to societal and systematic factors such as racial discrimination in the educational and legal system (Aymer, 2016; Chae et al., 2017; Matthews et al., 2013). Studies show that men, in general, engage in maladaptive coping such as substance use, more than women (Chae et al., 2017) and young men in college are less likely to utilize available mental health resources (Mincey et al., 2017) which can greatly impact their academic, psychological, and even physical functioning. Much like the discussion on sexual violence perpetrated on men (see Chapter 7), the gendered racism displayed dictates that any vulnerability expressed (physically, emotionally, psychologically) is an affront to a person's manhood must change. While it is commonplace to see student-led organizations on campus address mental health and psychological well-being through programming, more effort needs to be made to have organized and consistent support for young men. Creating and sustaining support-style groups on and off campus to address issues that are specific to them, and their needs will allow them a safe space to process and cope with their mental health. This is greatly needed on most HBCU campuses. If young men do talk about their mental health, it is often amongst their friends, teammates, and fraternity brothers. However, having consistent campus programming and outreach coupled with skilled leaders and facilitators may make a difference in the disclosure and treatment-seeking behavior of young Black men on campus.

Finally, it is of critical importance to consider the reality that sexual behavior is being used as a surrogate for other emotional and mental health issues among young Black college students. Based on the critical transitions that young people are making from high school to college campuses, coupled with sociocultural factors such as the gender-ratio imbalance (GRI), gender role conflict, pressure to conform on campuses, this connection is worthy of further consideration. One issue that students may be contending with is loneliness. Loneliness is defined by feelings and thoughts of being isolated and disconnected from others (Chang, 2018). Chang conducted a study with 168 Black college students (30.4% identified as men) and found that women reported higher scores on loneliness, anxiety, and depression measures. Additionally, all three measures were significantly correlated with each other. Loneliness has a documented relationship with sexual risk behavior mediated through increased alcohol and substance use, and in some instances, compulsive sexual behavior (Torres & Gore-Felton, 2007). Feelings of loneliness and despair increase the risk of using sexual activity as a coping mechanism (Cortoni & Marshall, 2001). It is because feelings of isolation and disconnectedness create negative emotional states and individuals look for opportunities to relieve these feelings. While there is not much literature available on this connection among young Black college students, it is worthy of further consideration. Edwards et al., (2017) found that 40% of participants, male and female, from an HBCU viewed sexual intercourse as a coping mechanism for stress related to work, school, and relationships. Sexual activity often provides a pleasurable experience to relieve these negative emotions; however, the coping mechanism is only a temporary fix like alcohol and substance use. Long-term strategies must include an understanding of how to address the underlying issues contributing to feelings of loneliness, isolation, and despair.

Alcohol and Substance Use

This psychosocial influence was saved for last, as it not only has a relationship with sexual health but with every other factor mentioned in this and other chapters. Some college students experience considerable peer pressure to use alcohol and/or substances (e.g., cigarettes/vape/ hookahs, illegal drugs, prescription drugs, inhalants, and solvents) particularly when trying to adjust to making friends and adapt to college life (Sawyer-Kurian & Wechsberg, 2012). The social context of universities – increased sexual opportunities, no parental oversight, an abundance of parties and events – contributes to the decision to drink alcohol and use substances (Perkins et al., 2020; Thorpe et al., 2020). While consuming alcohol is a concern, heavy and binge drinking is a *major* concern on many college campuses (Substance Abuse and Mental Health Services Administration [SAMHSA], 2018). Adverse consequences of alcohol use for college students (undergraduate and graduate) between the ages of 18 and 24 years include poor academic performance, physical injuries, difficulties within relationships, and poor psychological well-being. Many colleges, particularly those associated with religious institutions are often designated as 'dry campuses' which means alcohol cannot be served or consumed on the premises, regardless of age or event. Most of these campuses are in the Midwest and Southern states (The Economist, 2005), which is also where the majority of HBCUs are located. To be clear, having a university policy designating a campus as 'dry,' does not always translate into students not consuming alcohol on campus. In fact, it may serve as a mechanism for less formal monitoring because students who want to drink onsite will still find ways to do so. Students who reside in the dorms often have 'kick-back parties' in the rooms where each student brings beer and/or alcohol to share while socializing with each other. It is almost a certainty that most colleges, including those that prohibit alcohol on university property, have some variation of these types of parties. In contrast, 'wet campuses' permit the serving and consumption of alcohol to those of legal age, based on university policy. Some campuses are 'wet,' and it is commonplace to have beer and alcohol at events for the students who are of legal drinking age, staff, and faculty to consume.

Because alcohol and other substance use alter judgment and remove inhibitions, they engender high-risk sexual activity (Adefuye et al., 2009; Braby et al., 2020; Risi et al., 2019; Thomas et al., 2008). Research on alcohol and substance use in college students is heavily focused on White students, or students at PWIs; however, there has been some important work done with students attending HBCUs. The *2001 HBCU Substance Use Survey* by the National HBCU Substance Use Consortium surveyed students at over 30 HBCUs on their substance use and sexual behaviors. Using data from this survey, Browne et al. (2009) looked at 1837 male freshmen enrolled and found that consumption or use of alcohol and substances prior to sexual activity made them more prone to engage in risky sexual behaviors. Additionally, the young women in the Browne et al. study indicated that being under the influence of alcohol and/or other substances was the highest barrier to engaging in safer sex practices. Using the same dataset, Wang et al. (2011) reported a statistically significant finding that early sexual debut (before age 14) was moderately associated with onset of illegal substance use for the students in the survey. Students with early sexual experiences had higher use of illegal substances, compared to those without early sexual experiences. More recently, Heads et al. (2017) surveyed 398 Black students (African American and Afro-Caribbean) and found that men reported significantly higher rates of heavy drinking and risk behaviors such as casual sex, anal sex, and vaginal sex under the influence. The women in the study reported significantly higher rates of unprotected sexual activity. Jones et al. (2018) conducted a study with 150 HBCU students and found a statistically significant positive relationship between substance use and dependency and risky sexual behavior. Additionally, Hall and Jones (2020) found that those students who reported using more alcohol and substances, specifically marijuana, were more likely to have multiple partners in the past 12 months.

In addition to race/ethnicity and type of institution, research documents differences in sociodemographic variables such as gender and educational class are important for examining drinking patterns and subsequent sexual activity among college students (see Clarke et al., 2013). College-aged men typically engage in heavier daily and episodic drinking than college-aged women (Heads et al., 2017); however, the prevalence of heavy and binge drinking is becoming more equal between the genders (Lindong et al., 2017). There have been some empirical studies examining freshman, or first-year students and drinking patterns and behaviors such as the quantitative study by

Thorpe et al. (2020) investigating alcohol outcome expectancies and sexual risk. A sample of 307 Black freshman students from institutions around the United States participated in an online STI and alcohol prevention intervention study, and results indicate a lower percentage of students engaged in heavy drinking than the national average (7.5% vs. 42%). Additionally, there were no statistically significant relationship to sexual risk behaviors. Although most research indicates that Black students, particularly those at HBCUs (Hou, 2009), consume less alcohol than their White peers, the consequences of alcohol use appear to have more negative consequences.

The two most common substances used among young Black college students are alcohol and marijuana (Lindong et al., 2017), yet due to legal and political issues surrounding marijuana use, there has not been as much research done on its use by college students and its relationship with sexual activity. In a 2008 publication entitled *Alcohol and Other Drug Use at Historically Black Colleges and Universities* (Kapner, 2008), it was noted that the Center for Substance Abuse Treatment (CSAT) study done in the early 2000s with HBCU students showed that almost 15% of students had used marijuana within 30 days prior to the survey. A year later, Hayes et al. (2009) conducted a study with 1,115 freshmen from a consortium of HBCUs (52% male) and found that 17.7% of the participants had smoked marijuana in the past 30 days. Despite increased rates of marijuana use among youth and emerging adults, the empirical studies linking its use with sexual activity are limited. Most of the data is not with Black individuals; however, what is known is the positive relationship between marijuana and sexual risk behaviors and outcomes such as inconsistent condom use, STI infection and transmission, and multiple sexual partners (Berger et al., 2012; Bryan et al., 2012; Guo et al., 2002). More research on the use of marijuana by Black students at HBCUs is needed.

While alcohol and substance use put students at higher risk for poor decision-making and engagement in high-risk behavior, there have been numerous protective factors associated with HBCU attendance that helps curb these harmful outcomes. There is evidence that the culture of HBCUs, which heavily focuses on character and leadership development and provides a nurturing and supportive environment, discourages heavy and binge drinking and encourages adaptive coping strategies (Edwards et al., 2015; Meilman et al., 1995). Although HBCU students are engaging in less drinking and substance use than White students, the compounded effects of use should be concerning. Since young Black students have poorer sexual health outcomes, the clustering of alcohol and other substance use with sexual experiences must continue to be investigated. This provides more fodder for discussion around the development of prevention and intervention programs that focus on the strengths of HBCUs: pride, leadership, support, and family. Research and programming need to focus more on the connection between mental health, alcohol and substance use, and high-risk sexual behavior.

There is an adage that alcohol gives you 'liquid courage.' Liquid courage refers to using alcohol to engage in behaviors that you want to, but do not have the courage to do sober. In the realm of sexual activity, studies show that Black women have indicated using alcohol to increase pleasure, intensify the desire to give pleasure to a partner or partners, engage in a wider variety of sexual behaviors (some riskier than others), and to reduce guilt from hook-ups or casual relationships (Thorpe et al., 2020). Data also shows us that alcohol (and other substances) is also used as a justification to explore and/or engage in same-sex behaviors. For example, the sexual minority students in the Thorpe et al. study had significantly higher expectations of alcohol to increase their desire to take risks than the heterosexual-identified students. While sexual exploration is a normal part of development, the continued stigma around some identities, desires, and behaviors are still prevalent. There was a popular song back in 2009 by multi-dimensional artist Jamie Foxx entitled, *Blame it (Foxx, 2009)*. The song featured lyrics perfectly describing situations where alcohol was used as a scapegoat for behaviors. Foxx talked about how some blame 'booze' as a way to cover up the desire to engage in certain behaviors. The expectation of alcohol to alleviate inhibitions and create situations that allow students to engage in behaviors that may be frowned upon without alcohol can lead to disappointment and feelings of anguish. This can begin a cycle of drinking to combat these feelings but continuing to have these feelings because the outcome from drinking did not provide the anticipated outcome.

Finally, many studies document the adverse consequences of alcohol and other substance use and its relationship with high-risk sexual activity, but there needs to be more information on the issue of sexual consent. Alcohol and substance use alters one's body chemistry, which clouds judgment (Xu & Xu, 2018) and helps facilitate engagement in high-risk sexual activity that one may not have agreed to if sober. Therefore, one cannot appropriately consent to engagement in these activities; however, the increase of incapacitated sexual assault numbers on college campuses has increased (Palmer & St. Vil, 2018). More work must be done with what The Consent Academy (The Consent Academy, n.d.) calls 'capacity' consent. Students who are under the influence of alcohol and other substances that can alter one's capacity to think lucidly are often not able to provide a clearheaded response. Additionally, not asking but assuming is not consent. While every university that receives Federal funds has a Title IX Office or administrator, it is imperative to shift the focus (and resources) to prevention and intervention, and not simply punishment. It is possible that students are not sure what constitutes consent and how to ensure that it is obtained before engaging in sexual activity. The next chapter looks at social and cultural factors that are important to investigate, and understand, as it relates to sexual decision-making and subsequent behavior.

References

Adefuye, A. S., Abiona, T. C., Balogun, J. A., & Lokoro-Durrell, M. (2009). HIV sexual risk behaviors and perception of risk among college students: implications for planning interventions. *BMC Public Health*, *9*(1), 1–13.

Alvy, L. M., McKirnan, D. J., Mansergh, G., Koblin, B., Colfax, G. N., Flores, S. A., & Hudson, S. (2011). Depression is associated with sexual risk among men who have sex with men, but is mediated by cognitive escape and self-efficacy. *AIDS and Behavior*, *15*(6), 1171–1179.

Avery, L. R., Stanton, A. G., Ward, L. M., Cole, E. R., Trinh, S. L., & Jerald, M. C. (2021). "Pretty hurts": Acceptance of hegemonic feminine beauty ideals and reduced sexual well-being among Black women. *Body Image*, *38*, 181–190.

Aymer, S. R. (2016). "I can't breathe": A case study—Helping Black men cope with race-related trauma stemming from police killing and brutality. *Journal of Human Behavior in the Social Environment*, *26*(3-4), 367–376.

Berger, A. T., Khan, M. R., & Hemberg, J. L. (2012). Race differences in longitudinal associations between adolescent personal and peer marijuana use and adulthood sexually transmitted infection risk. *Journal of Addictive Diseases*, *31*(2), 130–142.

Boyd-Starke, K., Hill, O. W., Fife, J., & Whittington, M. (2011). Religiosity and HIV risk behaviors in African-American students. *Psychological Reports*, *108*(2), 528–536.

Braby, L., Holcomb, M., & Leonhard, C. (2020). Examining the relationship between ethnic identity, depression, and alcohol use among students at historically Black colleges/universities (HBCUs). *Journal of Ethnicity in Substance Abuse*, *21*(2), 621–637.

Browne, D. C., Clubb, P. A., Wang, Y., & Wagner, F. (2009). Drug use and high-risk sexual behaviors among African American men who have sex with men and men who have sex with women. *American Journal of Public Health*, *99*(6), 1062–1066.

Bryan, A. D., Schmiege, S. J., & Magnan, R. E. (2012). Marijuana use and risky sexual behavior among high-risk adolescents: Trajectories, risk factors, and event-level relationships. *Developmental Psychology*, *48*(5), 1429.

Chae, D. H., Powell, W. A., Nuru-Jeter, A. M., Smith-Bynum, M. A., Seaton, E. K., Forman, T. A.,... & Sellers, R.. (2017). The role of racial identity and implicit racial bias in self-reported racial discrimination: Implications for depression among African American men. *Journal of Black Psychology*, *43*(8), 789–812.

Chandler, R., Guillaume, D., Tesema, N., Paul, S., Ross, H., & Hernandez, N. D. (2021). Social and environmental influences on sexual behaviors of college Black women: Within group diversity between HBCU vs. PWI experiences. *Journal of Racial and Ethnic Health Disparities*, *8*(4), 852–862.

Chang, E. C. (2018). Relationship between loneliness and symptoms of anxiety and depression in African American men and women: Evidence for gender as a moderator. *Personality and Individual Differences*, *120*, 138–143.

Clarke, N., Kim, S. Y., White, H. R., Jiao, Y., & Mun, E. Y. (2013). Associations between alcohol use and alcohol-related negative consequences among Black and White college men and women. Journal of studies on alcohol and drugs, *74*(4), 521–531.

Coleman, T., Gabriel, K., Coleman, N., & Carmack, C. (2018). "Wrap It Up!" Discourse on condom use among African American college-attending men in the southern US. *Open Journal of Social Sciences*, *6*(12), 111–126.

Cortoni, F., & Marshall, W. L. (2001). Sex as a coping strategy and its relationship to juvenile sexual history and intimacy in sexual offenders. *Sexual Abuse: A Journal of Research and Treatment*, *13*(1), 27–43.

Crepaz, N., & Marks, G. (2001). Are negative affective states associated with HIV sexual risk behaviors? A meta-analytic review. *Health Psychology*, *20*(4), 291.

Crooks, N., King, B., & Tluczek, A. (2020). Protecting young Black female sexuality. *Culture, Health & Sexuality*, *22*(8), 871–886.

Edwards, C. L., Fowler, S., Green, M., Kupper, A., Patkar, A. A., Hill, L.... Robinson, E. (2015). Institutional prevention programs as predictors of binge drinking among Black Americans attending Historically Black Colleges and Universities (HBCUs). *Negro Educational Review*, *66*(1–4), 89–99.

Edwards, L. V., Lindong, I., Brown, L., Hawkins, A. S., Dennis, S., Fajobi, O.,... & Sydnor, K. D. (2017). None of us will get out of here alive: the intersection of perceived risk for HIV, risk behaviors and survival expectations among African American emerging adults. *Journal of Health Care for the Poor and Underserved*, *28*(2), 48–68.

Elifson, K. W., Klein, H., & Sterk, C. E. (2010). Predictors of unsafe sex among at-risk heterosexual women. *Women's Health & Urban Life: An International and Interdisciplinary Journal*, *9*(2), 80.

El Bcheraoui, C., Sutton, M. Y., Hardnett, F. P., & Jones, S. B. (2013). Patterns of condom use among students at historically Black colleges and universities: Implications for HIV prevention efforts among college-age young adults. *AIDS Care*, *25*(2), 186–193.

Foxx, J. (2009). Blame it (on the alcohol) [Song]. On *Intuition* [Album]. J. Records.

Giordano, A. L., Cashwell, C. S., Lankford, C., King, K., & Henson, R. K. (2017). Collegiate sexual addiction: Exploring religious coping and attachment. *Journal of Counseling & Development, 95*(2), 135–144.

Guo, J., Chung, I. J., Hill, K. G., Hawkins, J. D., Catalano, R. F., & Abbott, R. D. (2002). Developmental relationships between adolescent substance use and risky sexual behavior in young adulthood. *Journal of Adolescent Health, 31*(4), 354–362.

Graham, L. F., Aronson, R. E., McCoy, R., & Rhodes, S. D. (2016). Sexual relationships, sex communication, and condom use among heterosexual African-American male college students in the southeastern US. *Journal of Black Sexuality and Relationships, 2*(3), 49–73.

Hall, N. M., Dickens, D., Lee, A. K., Corneille, M., & Younge, S. N. (2020). Colorism and racial politics at Historically Black Colleges/Universities. In K. Woodson (Ed.), *Colorism then, now, & tomorrow: Redefining a global phenomenon, with implications for policy, research, and practice.* Santa Barbara, CA: Fielding University Press.

Hall, N. M., & Jones, J. M. (2020). Predictors of sexual risk among HBCU students: Implications for STI/HIV prevention and intervention. *Journal of Black Sexuality and Relationships, 6*(3), 71–92.

Hall, N. M., Lee, A. K., & Witherspoon, D. D. (2014). Factors influencing dating experiences among African American emerging adults. *Emerging Adulthood, 2*(3), 184–194. PMC4271313

Hall, W. J., Erausquin, J. T., Nichols, T. R., Tanner, A. E., & Brown-Jeffy, S. (2019). Relationship intentions, race, and gender: Student differences in condom use during hookups involving vaginal sex. Journal of American College Health, *67*(8), 733–742.

Hayes, B. D., Holliday, R. C., Wade, B. H., Trawick, C., Hodge, M., Caplan, L.,… & Satcher, D. (2009). A comprehensive examination of the health knowledge, attitudes and behaviors of students attending historically black colleges and universities. *Journal of Health Care for the Poor and Underserved, 20*(20), 69.

Heads, A. M., Dickson, J. W., & Asby, A. T. (2017). Correlates of HIV risk-taking behaviors among African-American college students: HIV knowledge and ethnic identity. *Journal of Health Care for the Poor and Underserved, 28*(2), 155–170.

Hou, S. I. (2009). HIV-related behaviors among black students attending Historically Black Colleges and Universities (HBCUs) versus white students attending a traditionally white institution (TWI). *AIDS Care, 21*(8), 1050–1057.

Jack, D. C. (1991). *Silencing the self: Women and depression.* Harvard University Press.

Jackson, J. M., Seth, P., DiClemente, R. J., & Lin, A. (2015). Association of depressive symptoms and substance use with risky sexual behavior and sexually transmitted infections among African American female adolescents seeking sexual health care. *American Journal of Public Health, 105*(10), 2137–2142.

Jerald, M. C., Cole, E. R., Ward, L. M., & Avery, L. R. (2017). Controlling images: How awareness of group stereotypes affects Black women's well-being. *Journal of Counseling Psychology, 64*(5), 487.

Johnson, A. B. (2006). Performance anxiety among African-American college students: Racial bias as a factor in social phobia. *Journal of College Student Psychotherapy, 20*(4), 31–38.

Johnson, J. M. (2017). Social norms, gender ratio imbalance, perceptions of risk, and the sexual behaviors of African American women at Historically Black Colleges and Universities. *Journal of African American Studies, 21*, 203–215. 10.1007/s12111-017-9354-8

Jones, B. T., Eaton, S., Livingston, J. N., & Cliette, G. E. (2018). Substance use, risky sexual behavior and delinquency among students at a historically Black college. Addict Drug Sensitize, 2(109), 53–59.

Kapner, D. A. (2008). Alcohol and other drug use at Historically Black Colleges and Universities. Infofacts/Resources. *Higher Education Center for Alcohol and Other Drug Abuse and Violence Prevention.* https://files.eric.ed.gov/fulltext/ED537617.pdf

Khan, M. R., Kaufman, J. S., Pence, B. W., Gaynes, B. N., Adimora, A. A., Weir, S. S., & Miller, W. C. (2009). Depression, sexually transmitted infection, and sexual risk behavior among young adults in the United States. *Archives of Pediatrics & Adolescent Medicine, 163*(7), 644–652.

Kogan, S. M., Brody, G. H., Gibbons, F. X., Murry, B. M., Cutrona, C. E., Simons, R....DiClemente, R. (2008). The influence of role status on risky sexual behavior among African Americans during the transition to adulthood. *Journal of Black Psychology, 34*(3), 399–420.

Lehrer, J. A., Shrier, L. A., Gortmaker, S., & Buka, S. (2006). Depressive symptoms as a longitudinal predictor of sexual risk behaviors among US middle and high school students. *Pediatrics, 118*(1), 189–200.

Lennon, C. A., Huedo-Medina, T. B., Gerwien, D. P., & Johnson, B. T. (2012). A role for depression in sexual risk reduction for women? A meta-analysis of HIV prevention trials with depression outcomes. Social Science & Medicine, 75(4), 688–698.

Leivo, D. N., Leonhard, C., Johnson, K., & Carlson, T. (2021). Relationship of high-risk sexual behaviors, sexual knowledge, and sexual satisfaction among African American college students: Toward a sex positive approach to STI prevention. *Sexuality & Culture, 26*(1), 154–175.

Lenning, E. (2017). Unapologetically queer in unapologetically Black spaces: Creating an inclusive HBCU campus. *Humboldt Journal of Social Relations, 39*, 283–293.

Lindong, I., Edwards, L., Dennis, S., & Fajobi, O. (2017). Similarities and differences matter: Considering the influence of gender on HIV prevention programs for young adults in an urban HBCU. *International Journal of Environmental Research and Public Health, 14*(2), 133.

Lipson, S. K., Kern, A., Eisenberg, D., & Breland-Noble, A. M. (2018). Mental health disparities among college students of color. *Journal of Adolescent Health*, *63*(3), 348–356.

MacDonald, D. A. (2000). Spirituality: Description, measurement, and relation to the five factor model of personality. *Journal of Personality*, *68*(1), 153–197.

Marks, L. R., & Çiftçi, A. (2019). Microaggressions and sexual risk behaviors in Black college women: A moderated mediation analysis. *Journal of Multicultural Counseling and Development*, *47*(2), 108–118.

Matthews, D. D., Hammond, W. P., Nuru-Jeter, A., Cole-Lewis, Y., & Melvin, T. (2013). Racial discrimination and depressive symptoms among African-American men: The mediating and moderating roles of masculine self-reliance and John Henryism. *Psychology of Men & Masculinity*, *14*(1), 35.

Mattis, J. S. (2000). African American women's definitions of spirituality and religiosity. *Journal of Black Psychology*, *26*(1), 101–122.

Mbiti, J. S. (1990). *African religions & philosophy*. Heinemann.

McKirnan, D. J., Ostrow, D. G., & Hope, B. (1996). Sex, drugs and escape: A psychological model of HIV-risk sexual behaviours. *AIDS Care*, *8*(6), 655–670.

McLaurin-Jones, T. L., Lashley, M. B., & Marshall, V. J. (2017). Using qualitative methods to understand perceptions of risk and condom use in African American college women: implications for sexual health promotion. *Health Education & Behavior*, *44*(5), 805–814.

Meilman, P. W., Presley, C. A., & Cashin, J. R. (1995). The sober social life at historically Black colleges. *Journal of Blacks in Higher Education*, 9, 98–100.

Miller, W. R., & Thoreson, C. E. (2003). Spirituality, religion, and health: An emerging research field. *American Psychologist*, *58*, 24–35

Mincey, K., Turner, B. L., Brown, A., & Maurice, S. (2017). Understanding barriers to healthy behaviors in black college men. *Journal of American College Health*, *65*(8), 567–574.

Mouzon, D. M., Taylor, R. J., Nguyen, A. W., & Chatters, L. M. (2016). Serious psychological distress among African Americans: Findings from the national survey of American life. *Journal of Community Psychology*, *44*(6), 765–780.

Norwood, C. R., & Zhang, Y. (2015). Condom attitudes and use among African American college women students. *Journal of Black Sexuality and Relationships*, *2*(1), 83–99.

Palmer, J. E., & St. Vil, N. M. (2018). Sexual assault disclosure by college women at Historically Black Colleges and Universities and Predominantly White Institutions. *NASPA Journal About Women in Higher Education*, *11*(1), 33–55.

Perkins, E. L., Chacon, F., Obizoba, C., Stennis, K. B., Wutoh, R., Madison, L., Wells, G., & Turner, D. (2020). Determinants of risky sexual behaviors in an HBCU community. *Journal of Mental Health and Social Behaviour*, *2*(1), 116. 10.33790/jmhsb1100116.

Poulson, R. L., Bradshaw, S. D., Huff, J. M., Peebles, L. L., & Hilton, D. B. (2008). Risky sex behaviors among African American college students: The influence of alcohol, marijuana, and religiosity. *North American Journal of Psychology*, *10*(3), 529–542.

Risi, M. M., Forkus, S. R., Roy, A., Laforge, R. G., Rossi, J. S., & Weiss, N. H. (2019). The mediating role of impulsivity between psychological distress and alcohol misuse among college students at a historically Black university. *Journal of Dual Diagnosis*, *15*(2), 95–104.

Sawyer-Kurian, K. M., & Wechsberg, W. M. (2012). Adapting an evidence-based HIV intervention for at-risk African American college women at Historically Black Colleges and Universities who use alcohol and drugs. *Sage Open*, *2*(4), 1–13, 2158244012464977.

Stokes, L. R., & Brody, L. R. (2019). Self-Silencing, but not sexual relationship power associated with condom use for Black college-aged women. *Behavioral Sciences*, *9*(2), 13.

Substance Abuse and Mental Health Services Administration (2018). *Key substance use and mental health indicators in the United States: Results from the 2017 National Survey on Drug Use and Health*. Rockville, MD: Center for Behavioral Health Statistics and Quality, SAMHSA. Retrieved from https://www.samhsa.gov/data/

The Consent Academy (n.d.). Consent complexities. Retrieved from: https://www.consent.academy/consent-complexities.html

The Economist (2005). Dry campuses: Booze control. Retrieved from: https://www.economist.com/node/3577274/print?Story_ID=3577274

Thomas, S. E., Randall, P. K., Book, S. W., & Randall, C. L. (2008). A complex relationship between co-occurring social anxiety and alcohol use disorders: What effect does treating social anxiety have on drinking? *Alcoholism: Clinical and Experimental Research*, *32*(1), 77–84.

Thomas, T. L., & Freeman, A. (2011). Project genesis: Self-reported religiosity and spirituality and sexual risk-taking in young African-American women attending a historically African-American college. *Journal of National Black Nurses Association*, *22*(1), 27.

Thompson-Robinson, M. V., Richter, D. L., Shegog, M. L., Weaver, M., Trahan, L., Sellers, D. B., & Brown, V. L. (2005). Perceptions of partner risk and influences on sexual decision-making for HIV prevention among students at historically black colleges and universities. *Journal of African American Studies*, *9*(2), 16–28.

Thorpe, S., Tanner, A. E., Ware, S., Guastaferro, K., Milroy, J. J., & Wyrick, D. L. (2020). Black first-year college students' alcohol outcome expectancies. *American Journal of Health Education*, *51*(2), 78–86.

Torres, H. L., & Gore-Felton, C. (2007). Compulsivity, substance use, and loneliness: The loneliness and sexual risk model (LSRM). *Sexual Addiction & Compulsivity*, *14*(1), 63–75.

64   *Psychosocial Influences on Sexual Health*

Turner, A. K., Latkin, C., Sonenstein, F., & Tandon, S. D. (2011). Psychiatric disorder symptoms, substance use, and sexual risk behavior among African-American out of school youth. *Drug and Alcohol Dependence, 115*(1-2), 67–73.

Wang, Y., Storr, C., Browne, D. C., & Wagner, F. A. (2011). Early sexual experience and later onset of illegal drug use among African American students on HBCU campuses. *Substance Use & Misuse, 46*(4), 543–551.

Washington, T. A., Wang, Y., & Browne, D. (2009). Difference in condom use among sexually active males at Historically Black Colleges and Universities. *Journal of American College Health, 57*(4), 411–418.

Williams, K. L., Russell, A., & Summerville, K. (2021). Centering Blackness: An examination of culturally-affirming pedagogy and practices enacted by HBCU administrators and faculty members. *Innovative Higher Education, 46*(6), 733–757.

Winston-Salem State University. (2021). Ramdition Fall 2021. Retrieved from: https://www.wssu.edu/academics/colleges-and-departments/university-college-and-lifelong-learning/ramdition/index.html

Xu, J., & Xu, J. (2018). Impact of alcohol use and drug use on STD/HIV-related sexual risk behaviors among African American college students. *Medical & Clinical Research, 3*(5), 1–5.

Yarber, W. L., & Sayad, B. W. (2018). *Human sexuality: Diversity in contemporary America* (10th edition). New York: McGraw Hill.

Younge, S. N., Corneille, M. A., Lyde, M., & Cannady, J. (2013). The paradox of risk: Historically Black college/university students and sexual health. *Journal of American College Health, 61*(5), 254–262.

Younge, S. N., Wade, B. H., Geter, A., Holliday, R. C., & Trawick, C. (2018). Condom attitudes and condom use among first year college men attending a historically Black institution. *American Journal of Health Studies, 33*(2), 80–88.

6 Sociocultural Influences on Sexual Health

The connection between social and cultural factors has an undeniable influence on sexual health and behaviors. Although there is a plethora of sociocultural influences documented in the literature, this section focuses on three that has consistently shown strong relationships with the sexual health of young Black college students: gender-ratio imbalance/partner availability on HBCU campuses, gender roles, masculinity, and the media.

The Gender-Ratio Imbalance/Partner Availability

The gender-ratio imbalance (GRI) and partner availability within Black communities has received a lot of attention in the media and in the literature on STIs and HIV. Although there is widespread concern in the Black community, the imbalance appears to be more pronounced in college settings (see Holland, 2009; Longmire-Avital & Reavis, 2015; Stackman et al., 2016; Younge et al., 2014). The GRI, for college campuses, is when there is a higher proportion of women on campus than men. Partner availability is an individual's perceptions of the availability of mates with whom to engage with in one's environment (Hall et al., 2014). With the disproportionate gender dynamics on most HBCU campuses, the GRI and partner availability among women (especially those who identify as heterosexual) can present challenging cultural and environmental concerns as it relates to decision-making and subsequent behavior of students (Johnson, 2017). Research demonstrates that the GRI contributes to power imbalances within relationships, rivalries, competition, and increased sexual risk behavior (see Hall & Jones, 2020; Hall et al., 2014; Johnson, 2017; Pittman et al., 2019; Younge et al., 2007). Except for Morehouse College (an all-male HBCU), Black women are the largest consumers of higher education on HBCU campuses. Before moving any further it

DOI: 10.4324/9781003180944-6

is important to note that the lower number of Black males on campus is not based on a lack of intellect, motivation, or aspiration. It is heavily based on the numerous personal, social, socioeconomic, and structural barriers that Black men face in the educational and legal systems that impact their presence in institutions of higher education (see Pittman et al., 2019). There is a long, storied history of bias, prejudice, discrimination, lack of support, and racism directed toward young Black men in K-12 systems across the nation that disenfranchise them and make the attainment of a college degree more difficult.

Although marital relationships are infrequent among young college students of all races/ethnicities (Winfield & Whaley, 2005), the desire to begin forming committed relationships is often cultivated during the undergraduate years. The *intimacy vs. isolation* phase of identity development (ages 19 to 40 years) focuses on exploring personal and intimate relationships. In this respect, college campuses serve as the 'market' for partners, both sexual and romantic (Uecker & Regnerus, 2010). Since traditional college students spend most of their time interacting with other students on campus, a sense of community is developed, and individuals tend to date those who live near them. However, the reality of many campuses is that the shortage of available partners may directly, or indirectly, influence engagement in riskier sexual behavior such as inconsistent condom use, partner concurrency, or multiple casual (or hook-up) partners (Hall et al., 2014; Pittman et al., 2019). Younge et al. (2014) explored partner availability among 19 young Black men at an HBCU in the southeastern US. Researchers found that the men noted the various benefits of having an 'abundance' of women on campus. Similarly, young men who identified as same-sex attracted (or same-gender-loving) found that the diverse environment supported exploring that attraction because of the large Black male population. As quoted in Younge et al.

"... with so many attractive men, it kind of makes me more interested in that aspect

[relationships with men] ... then there's so many different types of them [men]. So

it's like, well, maybe I could be happy with an educated black male like myself, but

it's not concrete."

In another study, among 57 undergraduate students at an HBCU, themes of partner availability, specifically GRI and *acceptability* were represented amongst the focus groups. The imbalance of more women to men led to rivalry, jealousy, aggression, and competition amongst women. Men were believed to have more perceived power in relationships, which ultimately affected their decision-making (Hall et al., 2014). Women perceived fewer available options for partners, and this contributed to the feeling of being in competition with other women on campus. While these feelings of competition appeared to be self-imposed, it manifested in women agreeing to engage in certain types of relationships (e.g., casual and hook-ups) even when they wanted something different. One woman in the study noted that *"...all the guys want a casual relationship ... you don't really have a choice"* (p.188). The competition amongst women for attention from some men was seen as advantageous for the young men because it increased their available partners. The issues of acceptability vs. availability were a re-occurring norm in the focus groups. Whether the acceptability standards are realistic or unrealistic at this developmental stage, the GRI and perceptions of partner availability are real and their impact on sexual attitudes, beliefs, and behaviors should not be under-estimated.

Stackman et al. (2016) examined the attitudes on partner availability of 387 Black college students at both HBCUs and PWIs and found that 62.5% of males at the HBCUs felt as if there were sufficient partners available in comparison to 33.1% of the female students. Two-thirds of the females (66.9%) felt that partner availability was insufficient. With the low percentage of available men on campus, what are young Black women who seek relationships with young Black men to do? An obvious response is to look for companionship off campus and through other means (e.g., social media, dating apps). Young women are also increasingly exploring same-sex desires and attractions. As discussed previously in Chapter 4, the need for an emotional connection and intimacy is a hallmark of emerging adult-hood. This is an important point to raise as it is not known whether young women would explore these desires and attractions if there were more eligible and available men on campus; however, this is an area in need of more in-depth inquiry.

The Stackman et al. study also examined attitudes toward inter-racial dating and found that Black men had more favorable attitudes toward interracial dating, and thereby increasing their pool of potential partners. Despite indicating that partner availability was low, Black women were still more unfavorable to interracial dating. There have been numerous studies demonstrating that Black women want same-race partners (Chambers & Kravitz, 2011; Dauria et al., 2015), along with studies showing that Black women are less desirable by other races (Boyd et al., 2020). The discrepancy in partner availability has several consequences, particularly for Black women interested in forming relationships with other Black men. Some of the negative consequences of the GRI are seen in its connection to self-silencing because of the desire to keep the relationship. Individuals who desire companionship may not advocate for themselves in fear of jeopardizing the relationship (Stokes & Brody, 2019). This may be especially true as Black women represent a larger portion of students in higher education than men, and as they ascend the educational ladder, many have reported a smaller group of available Black men (Dixon, 2009) with similar education. While this may all seem daunting, it presents a window of opportunity to talk about the formation and maintenance of healthy intimate relationships, how one decides which characteristics and traits are important in a mate, and the roles that one may choose to play or accept in relationships.

Gender Roles

Gender roles are beliefs regarding the specific tasks, personalities, and behaviors that men and women are 'expected' to embrace (Littlefield, 2003; Mahalik et al., 1998; Nguyen et al., 2010). Gender roles are different from gender identity (one's conceptualization of themselves, which is not always in line with their biological sex, or the sex assigned to them at birth) and gender expression (one's external appearance expressed by clothing, hair, and pronoun choice). Gender roles are necessary to investigate as it relates to sexual health because identifying who we are, and how we should behave, ultimately dictates how we take care of ourselves. Gender roles influence and sometimes define the behavior and the interpersonal relationships of individuals (Ehrhardt & Wasserheit, 1991). In the context of sexual health, gender-related dynamics are relevant to whether an individual will take an active or passive role in sexual situations including, but not limited to, initiating discussions with a sexual partner about safer sex practices, deciding whether and when safer sex practices will occur, using strategies to negotiate or assert power to protect their own health, or refusing to engage in risky sexual practices (Bowleg et al., 2000). For example, 'traditional' gender roles emphasize passivity and submissiveness of women and is seen as a potential barrier to condom use in heterosexual relationships (Amaro, 1995). On the other hand, 'traditional' gender roles for men emphasize dominance, aggressiveness, and competitiveness. The term 'traditional' is used as most gender role scales and measurements used to assess gender roles are based on the experiences of White populations, and neglects the social, political, and historical oppression that Black people endure. Therefore, these heavily used scales may be limited since Black people tend to dis-identify with the *traditional* gender role binary and have their own distinct understanding of gender.

There is fluidity in gender and gender roles that may not conform to societies or a particular culture or subculture's normative view. Those students who have the audacity to be authentic in their identity and expression are often ostracized and in certain situations, punished. As indicated in the *Introduction,* the lively, energetic campus culture at HBCUs is palpable. There are so many different opportunities for character, professional, and leadership development of the students. One of these opportunities focus on student organizational activities such as campus Queen and/or King (Miss X and Mr. X). Each year students compete to represent their institution on and off campus. These are highly coveted positions in which students are expected to represent the university 'appropriately.' Many other organizations, including fraternities and sororities also crown a Miss and/or a Mr. X to serve in positions and act as ambassadors for that organization. While these are undoubtedly wonderful opportunities for the students, they are also steeped in 'traditional' gender roles and expectations. Students who do not identify on the gender binary, or their gender presentation may not be in line with the expected appearance of those who occupy those positions are often excluded (Ford, 2015). What is seen in these types of opportunities around campus is a strict adherence to rigid gender roles and expression and heteronormativity (belief that heterosexuality is the 'normal' or default sexuality). McCune (2014) suggested that the hegemonic gender roles supported can foster a culture of 'passing' by students as heterosexual to avert the stigma and feel part of the campus community. In the HBCU context, "the politics of passing as heterosexual can cause identity confusion for students, yet this politic is enacted as a means of survival and persistence in college" (Patton et al., 2020, p. 6). Hopefully, there are flashbacks from Chapter 2's discussion about the politics of respectability and their creation as a means for survival. Environments are being created and maintained that inspire and facilitate dissonance amongst young people. It is a vicious cycle that needs to end, along with antiquated beliefs about how students should express their identities.

Factors such as gender roles, gender role attitudes (beliefs about appropriate behaviors and roles), gender role stereotypes (rigid, oversimplified, and overgeneralized beliefs about how gender should be expressed), and gender role conflict (psychological distress caused by rigid adherence to traditional masculine norms) influence how individuals take care of themselves and others. Some researchers posit that some Black people are conflicted about their cultural ideas about gender and roles versus society's norms (i.e., Eurocentric) about gender and roles. Gendered-racial stereotypes are generalizations made about African American men and women that are derived from their historical and gender-specific experiences of oppression (Jones et al., 2018). This may create gender role conflict and discord within the family. For instance, hegemonic masculinity asserts that men should display certain characteristics and be the breadwinners in the household. However, systematic oppression limits the ability of many Black men to fulfill that role (see Collins, 1998) in the same way as White men have done in the past. Additionally, because of the history of slavery in the United States, Black women, unlike women of other races, have always worked outside of the home and were responsible for contributing financially to the household.

More than two decades of data shows us that gender roles and gender role attitudes significantly contribute to disproportionate rates of unplanned pregnancies, STI, and HIV infection in Black women (Wingood & DiClemente, 2006; Wyatt, 2009). Studies also show that women who adhere to traditional gender norms are more likely to engage in behaviors that increase their risk of contracting HIV (Campbell, 1995; Pleck et al.,1993; Sikkema et al., 2000; Wingood & DiClemente, 1997). Consideration of the socially and culturally de-fined gender role context is essential in understanding sexual attitudes, decision-making, and behavior (Amaro, 1995). For example, Amaro argued that within heterosexual women's ascribed gender roles, sex is something that women give to men, leaving little room for women's acceptance of their own sexuality. For men, researchers noted that African American men were challenged with reconciling their man-hood with Eurocentric ideals, thereby contributing to the potential for gender role conflict or ambivalence.

There are numerous influences on how people learn about gender roles; however, peers and the media are extremely influential for Black emer-ging adults. A person's peer group provides information about gender role norms, and they influence the adoption of the norms through verbal approval or disapproval. That information is integrated into one's self-schema and eventually their sexual schema and acted upon through sexual scripts. If the norms of one's friendship group are that "good girls don't carry condoms" or "real men are always ready for sex" that is what the individual will subsequently enact. The media sends messages about gender, gender roles, sex, sexuality, and masculinity through advertisements, images, music, and programming. More about the media influences in the Media section below.

Masculinities

Sexual health outcomes for young Black men in college remain disproportionately worse than students of other racial/ethnic groups (Buhi et al., 2010; Centers for Disease Control and Prevention, 2019; Younge et al., 2018). Young Black men (ages 15–24) have disparate STI incidence and prevalence rates compared to men of other racial groups (Centers for Disease Control and Prevention, 2019), and those attending college, especially those attending HBCUs are at increased risk for poorer sexual health outcomes (Hall et al., 2014; Mincey et al., 2017). For example, available evidence of sexual behavior at HBCUs found high rates of oral and vaginal sex (Bazargan et al., 2000; Hou, 2009; Thomas et al., 2008), unprotected anal sex (Hou, 2009), inconsistent condom use (Thomas et al., 2008; Sutton et al., 2011; Younge et al., 2018), sexual activity under the influence of alcohol and/or marijuana (Buhi et al., 2010; Pass et al., 2016), having multiple sexual partners (Thomas et al., 2015), and higher likelihood to have an unintentional pregnancy (Hou, 2009). Recent attention has been given to the concept of multiple masculinities as a construct that might help us to understand these sexual health disparities in this population. Masculinities are socially constructed and influenced enactments of manhood (Alexander, 2006; Connell & Messerschmidt, 2005; Dancy, 2012; Mankowski & Maton, 2010). Men 'enact' different masculinities in different social contexts (Butler, 1990; Harris, 2010) to make others aware of the varying ideas/ideals of what it is to be a man (Hunter & Davis, 1992). For example, scholars are paying increased attention to the health implications of these gendered expectations and normative gender roles (e.g., 'hypermasculinity') on men's health, especially how they are associated with health behaviors and sexual practices (Courtenay, 2002) that can enhance sexual health risks (Haslam et al., 2009), and contribute to the observed health disparities (Griffin, 2012).

The HBCU context interacts with Black masculine ideals in ways that affect young Black men's sexual health. Many of the gendered barriers to men's health behavior may have to do with how men psychologically and behaviorally cope with being in an environment where they are under pressure to fulfill key social and cultural roles (Bowleg et al., 2013; Courtenay, 2002; Griffin, 2012). Qualitative studies with heterosexual men at HBCUs identified several factors that placed men at higher risk for contracting STIs. Two of the main factors included a gender ratio imbalance that favors men (on some

HBCU campuses the imbalance is as high as 75% women and 25% men) and having a small network to choose from for sexual partners (Hall & Applewhite, 2013; Hall & Witherspoon, 2011; Mincey et al., 2017). When contrasted with the GRI from women's perspective, one sees that they are operating on opposite sides of the same coin but both having deleterious outcomes.

The HBCU cultural context is an excellent environment to study enacted masculinities among young Black men. HBCUs are racially homogenous, but culturally diverse environments focused on leadership development and Black upward mobility (Grundy, 2012; Treadwell et al., 2009). Because of this focus, young Black men attending HBCUs are perceived to have greater access to fulfilling 'traditional' or mainstream masculinities (e.g., financial and career success) (Cazenave, 1981). Additionally, they are also thought to have more freedom to reject stereotypical masculinities such as 'hypermasculinity' that may place them at increased risk for poorer health outcomes such as STIs (Aronson et al., 2013; Levant et al., 1998; Wade, 2009). Most HBCUs were founded with strong religious connections, and these legacies are enduring and contribute to the construction, enactment, and performance of various masculinities (Wade, 2009). HBCUs can be nurturing, welcoming, and inclusive for young Black men; however, they may also produce psychological distress in those whose masculinities may be counter to the overall conservative culture of the campus. HBCUs can be spaces where Black male students' gender, racial, and sexual identities conflict with the campus culture (Mobley & Hall, 2020). Njoku et al. (2017) note that the 'privilege' of Black men in certain capacities at HBCUs also results in being heavily regulated and constrained by some would say, antiquated beliefs about gender roles, presentation, and masculinity. For instance, some young Black men may feel that engaging in same-sex behaviors are a threat to Black masculinity, which is consistent with the cultural norms on which many HBCUs were established. How will students reconcile this? Are there support systems on campus to help assist the student? Navigating this duality may have important implications that need to be investigated further.

Many young Black men at PWIs encounter the same pressure to conform to a particular type of gender expression and/or masculinity. Strayhorn and Tillman-Kelly (2013) conducted a study with 29 Black gay-identified men in college to investigate constructions of manhood and masculine identities and how these beliefs affected their experiences. Their findings revealed that participants understood their masculine identities in one of three ways. First, reproducing traditionally masculine behaviors was seen as participants repeatedly used heteronormative words to describe what it means to be a Black man. They also talked about 'performance' which included potentially dating and/or having sexual encounters with women to prove themselves as a 'real man.' In other words, 'passing' as discussed earlier in this chapter. Secondly, subverting hegemonic masculinities through intentional actions, such as engaging in activities traditionally viewed as feminine or less masculine. These activities could include presenting oneself as 'extra' and 'over the top.' The young men who spoke about this understood these actions may result, or have resulted, in being stigmatized and alienated by some other same-race men on campus. Finally, acknowledging that their masculinities were informed by their social locations. The intersection of this identity and location is informed by race, gender, class, and religion, and affected their sexuality and sexual behavior. More research is needed to understand the construction of masculinities and how do they manifest in sexual experiences on different campus cultural contexts.

Media

Media may be the most influential, and powerful, socializing agent for Black emerging adults. Depictions of sex and sexuality in the media are sometimes meant to educate, but most often to entertain and exploit, therefore they do not always contain accurate depictions of sexuality or behavior (Yarber & Sayad, 2018). Media is represented in numerous modalities including television shows, web shows, movies, music, websites, and social media platforms, such as Instagram and Twitter. College students are inundated by media and exposure daily (Chandler et al., 2021). Coyne et al., (2013) noted that one of the most salient features of emerging adulthood is the extensive use of media. On average, college students spend close to half of the day using some form of media. Current students have unprecedented access to media through technological advances such as streaming services. With the amount of time college students spend accessing media, researchers claim they are 'media saturated' (Vandewater et al., 2007) and Black students spend more time utilizing media than other groups (Matabane & Merritt, 2014). Although media serves as a source of information and influence, it may also serve as a negative influence on the sexual health for Black individuals. The media may operate as a threat to intimacy for Black individuals because of its racialized and gendered stereotypes about the sexuality and behaviors of Black men and women (Helm & Carlson, 2013; Dogan et al., 2018). For example, anti-Black narratives often portray Black men and women as hypersexual and without concern for, or appreciation of intimacy and/ or loving relationships. One section of a chapter cannot fully illuminate the influence media has on the overall sexual health and wellbeing of Black college students attending HBCUs. This is just meant to introduce media as a sociocultural influence. Therefore, the decision was made to focus on one modality, music, as an influencing factor on the sexual health and sexual health outcomes of Black college students.

There have been recent studies focused on the overwhelming impact of two musical genres, *R&B* (Rhythm & Blues) and *Hip-Hop/Rap*, on college campuses and its influence on the sexual health and sexual health outcomes of young Black college students. The R&B and Hip-Hop genres have produced songs with high levels of sexual content over the years. Lyrics range from songs about intimacy to love to raw sexual references. Chandler et al. (2021) implemented an HIV prevention intervention for Black college women attending HBCUs and PWIs entitled, *The Health Improvement Project for LADIES* (HIP Ladies). A total of 63 participants completed a descriptive cross-sectional survey designed to collect baseline data on what they saw as major influences on their sexual behavior. Results indicated that music had a significantly stronger influence on sexuality and sexual behaviors of the women who attended the HBCU than those at the PWIs. HBCU students also significantly agreed that the content of the songs frequently gave instruction on how they 'should' engage sexually. These findings are in line with previous research demonstrating a connection between sexual content in music and engagement in riskier sexual activity, such as with multiple partners, partner concurrency, and inconsistent or no condom use (Wright & Craske, 2015).

Available evidence indicates that Black men, in terms of media engagement, were primarily interested in musical content (Goodwill et al., 2019; The Opportunity Agenda, 2011). Hip hop, as a culture, is thought to be more appealing to younger men and women, particularly young Black men. As a critical element of the hip hop culture, rap music has expanded its brand as a commercial entity with representations of Black men, and masculinities, globally in several media outlets such as magazines, music, television shows, film, and websites (see Alonso-Recarte, 2020; Avery et al., 2017; Belle, 2014; Boylorn, 2017). Through a content analysis of masculine representations in 527 songs of *Billboard Magazine's Hot 100* and *Billboard's Hot R&B/Hip-Hop* year-end charts of Black artists from the years 1990 to 2010, themes of material goods as status, competition, controlling emotions, violent behaviors, risk-taking, survival, homophobia, anti-femininity, dominance, focusing on sex, being a hero/financial provider, confrontation, and questioning the masculinity of other men, were found (Avery et al., 2017). Contemporary R&B culture has continued to represent a more fluid sense of masculinity and what it means to be a man. Frank Ocean is an alternative R&B artist that has represented a diverse array of Black masculinities in the public eye. In his album *Channel Orange,* his song entitled 'Thinking Bout You' is the story of a male finding love for the first time in another male. At one point, he illustrates a demeanor that may be perceived as more hypermasculine because he sings about money and material items and dismisses a kiss between the two, then switches to a more vulnerable tone when he sings about remaining together forever and being in love with the person during the chorus (Dhaenens & De Ridder, 2015).

The rapper, Young Thug, whose real name is Jeffrey Williams, has been called a rap iconoclast by GQ Magazine (Coley, 2019). He challenged traditional views of masculinity, and Black masculinity specifically, by posing not only in a dress but a dress that was described as 'billowing' for his 2016 release. His outward gender fluidity and refusal to be placed in a binary box have caused an uproar in a culture (Hip-Hop) that may be seen by many as *the* representative of gender norms in society. Some rap artists and their lyrical content objectify women, some portray an image of hypermasculinity, and some do neither and focus more on political messages about uplifting the community. It has been said that Hip-Hop may be one of the most, if not the most, diverse genres of music available. Even with Young Thug there are still contradictions, like with Frank Ocean. He is on the cover in a dress, yet in a 2019 interview he said, *"I wore this long-ass dress because I had a motherfu**ing AK-47 up under it."*

More recently, Lil Nas X, an openly same-gender-loving young Black male rose to fame with his internationally acclaimed song, 'Old Town Road.' Although he has released more music since his 2018 debut, what appears to be much of the fodder for discussion is his outward expressions of sexuality. When Lil Nas X was asked about his perspective on homophobia in Hip-Hop in a 2021 interview with NPR (Madden, 2021), he said

> *"I wouldn't be here without hip-hop. I understand how things have been, and I let go of it, you know? Like, there's a long build of homophobia not even just in hip-hop but, like, in the world. It's, like, something that has been molded for a very long time, and I understand that it takes a lot for people to unlearn, you know?"*

He, like many other young Black men can understand, acknowledge, and respect the culture of Hip-Hop and its influence, while also challenging the historical norms and beliefs.

A manuscript from a recently completed study is currently under review by a collaborative team lead by the book's author. The manuscript focuses on the influence of music on the construction and enactment of masculinities of young Black men attending HBCUs. Participants included 23 male and female students from two neighboring HBCUs. A major theme identified was the power and impact of song lyrics and lifestyle representation of the musical artists who sing R&B or rap them. Overwhelmingly, most of the young Black men listened to and referred to R&B and rap artists as being extremely influential in their identity development and conceptions and enactments of masculinities. The YBM discussed several different musical figures whose public personas are seen as influential enough to either emulate or to use as a 'cautionary tale.'

Findings from all of these studies should be used to elucidate the importance of further investigating how young Black college students are influenced by musical lyrics, artists, images, and messages from other Black people in entertainment. While it is important to say that *representation matters*, more research needs to be done on *how* it matters, *why* it matters, and *what* impact it has on the sexual health and sexual health outcomes of young Black men and women. Because Black emerging adults are frequent and consistent consumers of rap music and fervent supporters of rappers and Hip-Hop culture (Coyne et al., 2013), it is a culturally responsive approach to utilize this in university programming and activities. Through culturally responsive programming, students can learn how to distinguish between representation or messages for entertainment or shock value, versus those that are rooted in accurate information and positivity.

References

Alexander, B. K. (2006). *Performing Black masculinity: Race, culture, and queer identity*. AltaMira.

Alonso-Recarte, C. (2020). Pit bulls and dogfighting as symbols of masculinity in hip hop Culture. *Men and Masculinities, 23*(5), 852–871.

Amaro, H. (1995). Love, sex, power: Considering women's realities in HIV prevention. *American Psychologist, 50*, 437–447

Aronson, R. E., Rulison, K. L., Graham, L. F., Pulliam, R. M., McGee, W. L. Labban, J. D., Dingman, D., & Rhodes, S. D. (2013). Brothers leading healthy lives: Outcomes from the pilot testing of a culturally and contextually congruent HIV prevention intervention for Black male college students. *AIDS Education and Prevention, 25*(5), 376–393. 10.1521/aeap.2 013.25.5.376

Avery, L. R., Ward, L. M., Moss, L., & Üsküp, D. (2017). Tuning gender: Representations of femininity and masculinity in popular music by Black artists. *Journal of Black Psychology, 43*(2), 159–191. 10.1177/009579841562 7917

Bazargan, M., Kelly, E. M., Stein, J. A., Husaini, B. A., & Bazargan, S. H. (2000). Correlates of HIV risk-taking behaviors among African-American college students: The effect of HIV knowledge, motivation, and behavioral skills. *Journal of the National Medical Association, 92*(8), 391–404.

Belle, C. (2014). From Jay-Z to Dead Prez: Examining representations of Black masculinity in mainstream versus underground hip-hop music. *Journal of Black Studies, 45*(4), 287–300.

Bowleg, L., Belgrave, F. Z., & Reisen, C. A. (2000). Gender roles, power strategies, and precautionary sexual self-efficacy: Implications for Black and Latina women's HIV/AIDS protective behaviors. *Sex Roles, 42*, 613–636.

Bowleg, L., Teti, M., Malebranche, D. J., & Tschann, J. M. (2013). "It's an uphill battle everyday": Intersectionality, low-income Black heterosexual men, and implications for HIV prevention research and interventions. *Psychology of Men and Masculinities, 14*(1), 25–34. 10.1037/a0028392

Boyd, B., Stephens, D. P., Eaton, A., & Bruk-Lee, V. (2020). Exploring partner scarcity: Highly educated black women and dating compromise. *Sexuality Research and Social Policy, 4*, 1–13.

Boylorn, R. M. (2017). From boys to men: Hip-hop, hood films, and the performance of contemporary Black masculinity. *Black Camera, 8*(2), 146–164. 10.2979/blackcamera.8.2.09

Buhi, E. R., Marhefka, S. L., & Hoban, M. T. (2010). The state of the union: Sexual health disparities in a national sample of US college students. *Journal of American College Health, 58*(4), 337–346. 10.1080/07448480903501780

Butler, J. (1990). Performative acts and gender constitution: An essay in phenomenology and feminist theory. In S. E. Case (Ed.), *Performing feminism: Feminist critical theory and theatre* (pp. 270–282). Johns Hopkins University.

Campbell, C. A. (1995). Male gender roles and sexuality: Implications for women's AIDS risk and prevention. *Social Science and Medicine, 41*, 197–210.

Cazenave, N. A. (1981). Black men in America: The quest for "manhood." In H. P. McAdoo (Ed.), Black families (pp. 176–186). Beverly Hills, CA: Sage.

Centers for Disease Control and Prevention. (2019, June). *Sexual Health.* National Center for HIV/AIDS, Viral Hepatitis, STD, and TB Prevention. https://www.cdc.gov/sexualhealth/Default.html

Chambers, A. L., & Kravitz, A. (2011) Understanding the disproportionately low marriage rate among African Americans: An amalgam of sociological and psychological constraints. *Family Relations, 60*(5), 648–660.

Chandler, R., Guillaume, D., Tesema, N., Paul, S., Ross, H., & Hernandez, N. D. (2021). Social and environmental influences on sexual behaviors of college Black women: Within group diversity between HBCU vs. PWI experiences. *Journal of Racial and Ethnic Health Disparities, 8*(4), 852–862.

Coley, J. (August 27, 2019). Young Thug is giving you what you want to hear. GQ Magazine. Retrieved from: https://www.gq.com/story/young-thug-is-giving-you-what-you-want-to-hear

Collins, P. H. (1998). Intersections of race, class, gender, and nation: Some implications for Black family studies. *Journal of Comparative Family Studies*, *29*(1), 27–36.

Connell, R. W., & Messerschmidt, J. W. (2005). Hegemonic masculinity: Rethinking the concept. Gender & society, *19*(6), 829–859.

Courtenay, W. H. (2002). A global perspective on the field of men's health: An editorial. *International Journal of Men's Health*, *1*(1), 1–13. 10.3149/jmh.0101.1

Coyne, S. M., Padilla-Walker, L. M., & Howard, E. (2013). Emerging in a digital world: A decade review of media use, effects, and gratifications in emerging adulthood. *Emerging Adulthood*, *1*(2), 125–137.

Dancy, T. E. (2012). *The brother code: Manhood and masculinity among African American males in college*. Information Age Publishing.

Dauria, E. F., Oakley, L., Arriola, K. J., Elifson, K., Wingood, G., & Cooper, H. L. (2015). Collateral consequences: Implications of male incarceration rates, imbalanced sex ratios and partner availability for heterosexual Black women. *Culture, Health & Sexuality*, *17*(10), 1190–1206. 10.1080/13691058.2015.1045035

Dhaenens, F., & De Ridder, S. (2015). Resistant masculinities in alternative R&B? Understanding Frank Ocean and The Weeknd's representations of gender. *European Journal of Cultural Studies*, *18*(3), 283–299.

Dixon, P. (2009). Marriage among African Americans: What does the research reveal? *Journal of African American Studies*, *13*, 29–46. 10.1007/s12111-008-9062-5

Dogan, J., Hargons, C., Meiller, C., Oluokun, J., Montique, C., & Malone, N. (2018). Catchin' feelings: Experiences of intimacy during Black college students' sexual encounters. *Journal of Black Sexuality and Relationships*, *5*(2), 81.

Ehrhardt, A. A., & Wasserheit, J. N. (1991). Age, gender and sexual risk behaviors for sexually transmitted diseases in the United States. In J. N. Wasserheit, S. O. Aral. K. K. Holmes, & P. J. Hitchcock (Eds.), *Research issues in human behavior and sexually transmitted diseases in the AIDS era* (pp. 97–121). Washington, DC: American Society for Microbiology.

Ford, O., III. (2015). From navigation to negotiation: An examination of the lived experiences of Black gay male alumni of historically black colleges and universities. *Journal of Homosexuality*, *62*(3), 353–373.

Goodwill, J. R., Anyiwo, N., Williams, E. D. G., Johnson, N. C., Mattis, J. S., & Watkins, D. C. (2019). Media representations of popular culture figures and the construction of Black masculinities. *Psychology of Men & Masculinities*, *20*(3), 288–298. 10.1037/men0000164

Griffin, D. M. (2012). An intersectional approach to men's health. *Journal of Men's Health*, *9*(2), 106–112. 10.1016/j.jomh.2012.03.003

Grundy, S. (2012). "An air of expectancy:" Class, crisis, and the making of manhood at a historically Black college for men. *The Annals of the American*

Academy of Political and Social Science, 642(1), 43–60. 10.1177%2F000271
6212438203

Hall, N. M., & Applewhite, S. (2013). Masculine ideology, norms, and HIV
prevention among young Black men. *Journal of HIV/AIDS & Social
Services, 12*, 384–403.

Hall, N. M., & Jones, J. M. (2020). Predictors of sexual risk among HBCU
students: Implications for STI/HIV prevention and intervention. *Journal of
Black Sexuality and Relationships, 6*(3), 71–92.

Hall, N. M., Lee, A. K., & Witherspoon, D. D. (2014). Factors influencing
dating experiences among African American emerging adults. *Emerging
Adulthood, 2*(3), 184–194. PMC4271313

Hall, N. M., Peterson, J. & Johnson, M. (2014). To test or not to test: Barriers
and solutions to testing African American college students for HIV at a
historically Black college. *Journal of Health Disparities Research and
Practice, 7*(1), 1–15. PMC4271312.

Hall, N. M., & Witherspoon, D. D. (2011). The influence of sociosexuality and
perceived susceptibility on the sexual behavior of African American college
students. *Journal of Best Practices in Health Professions Diversity: Research,
Education, and Policy, 4*(2), 681–697.

Harris, F. (2010). College men's meanings of masculinities and contextual
influences. Toward a conceptual model. *Journal of College Student
Development, 51*(3), 297–318. 10.1353/csd.0.0132

Haslam, S. A., Jetten, J., Postmes, T., & Haslam, C. (2009). Social identity,
health, and well-being: An emerging agenda for applied psychology. *Applied
Psychology: An International Review, 58*(1), 1–23. 10.1111/j.1464-0597.2
008.00379.x

Helm, K. M., & Carlson, J. (Eds.). (2013). *Love, intimacy, and the African
American couple*. Routledge.

Holland, R. (2009). Perceptions of mate selection for marriage among African
American, college-educated, single mothers. *Journal of Counseling &
Development, 87*(2), 170–178.

Hou, S. I. (2009). HIV-related behaviors among black students attending
Historically Black Colleges and Universities (HBCUs) versus white students
attending a traditionally white institution (TWI). *Aids Care, 21*(8), 1050–1057.

Hunter, A. G., & Davis, J. E. (1992). Constructing gender: An exploration of
African American men's conceptualization of manhood. *Gender & Society,
6*(3), 464–479. 10.1177%2F089124392006003007

Johnson, J. M. (2017). Social norms, gender ratio imbalance, perceptions of
risk, and the sexual behaviors of African American women at Historically
Black Colleges and Universities. *Journal of African American Studies, 21*,
203–215. 10.1007/s12111-017-9354-8

Jones, M. K., Buque, M., & Miville, M. L. (2018). African American gender
roles: A content analysis of empirical research from 1981 to 2017. *Journal of
Black Psychology, 44*(5), 450–486. 10.1177/0095798418783561

Levant, R. F., Majors, R. G., & Kelley, M. L. (1998). Masculinity ideology among young African American and European American women and men in different regions of the United States. *Cultural Diversity and Mental Health, 4*(3), 227.

Littlefield, M. B. (2003). Gender role identity and stress in African American women. *Journal of Human Behavior in the Social Environment, 8,* 93–104.

Longmire-Avital, B., & Miller-Dyce, C. (2015). Factors related to perceived status in the campus community for first generation students at an HBCU. *College Student Journal, 49*(3), 375–386.

Madden, S. (Host). (2021, September 21). Lil' Nax X is not trying to comfort anyone. [Audio podcast episode]. In *Consider This from NPR*. National Public Radio, Inc. https://www.npr.org/2021/09/23/1040187962/lil-nas-x-is-not-trying-to-comfort-anyone

Mahalik, J. R., Good, G. E., & Englar-Carlson, M. (2003). Masculinity scripts, presenting concerns, and help seeking: Implications for practice and training. *Professional Psychology: Research and Practice, 34*(2), 123.

Mahalik, J. R., Cournoyer, R. J., DeFranc, W., Cherry, M., & Napolitano, J. M. (1998). Men's gender role conflict and use of psychological defenses. Journal of Counseling Psychology, *45*(3), 247.

Mankowski, E. S., & Maton, K. L. (2010). A community psychology of men and masculinity: Historical and conceptual review. *American Journal of Community Psychology, 45,* 73–86. 10.1007/s10464-009-9288-y

Matabane, P. W., & Merritt, B. D. (2014). Media use, gender, and African American college attendance: The Cosby effect. *Howard Journal of Communications, 25*(4), 452–471.

McCune, J. R. (2014). *Sexual discretion: Black masculinity and the politics of passing.* The University of Chicago Press.

Mincey, K., Turner, B. L., Brown, A., & Maurice, S. (2017). Understanding barriers to healthy behaviors in black college men. *Journal of American College Health, 65*(8), 567–574.

Mobley Jr, S. D., & Hall, L. (2020). (Re) Defining queer and trans* student retention and "success" at Historically Black Colleges and Universities. *Journal of College Student Retention: Research, Theory & Practice, 21*(4), 497–519.

Nguyen, A. B., Clark, T. T., Hood, K. B., Corneille, M. A., Fitzgerald, A. Y., & Belgrave, F. Z. (2010). Beyond traditional gender roles and identity: Does reconceptualization better predict condom-related outcomes for African American women? *Culture, Health & Sexuality, 12,* 603–617.

Njoku, N., Butler, M., & Beatty, C. C. (2017). Reimagining the historically Black college and university (HBCU) environment: Exposing race secrets and the binding chains of respectability and othermothering. *International Journal of Qualitative Studies in Education, 30*(8), 783–799.

Pass, K. M., Younge, S. N., Geter, A., Al-Bayan, M., & Wade, B. H. (2016). A qualitative analysis of emerging adult Black men's sexual decision-making behavior and substance use. *Journal of Ethnicity in Substance Abuse, 15*(4), 386–404. 10.1080/15332640.2015.1064053103

Patton, L. D., Blockett, R. A., & McGowan, B. L. (2020). Complexities and contradictions: Black lesbian, gay, bisexual, and queer students' lived realities across three urban HBCU contexts. *Urban Education*, 0042085920959128.

Pittman, D. M., Kaur, P., & Eyler, L. T. (2019). Hidden in plain sight: Making a case for heterosexual Black college women being identified as a high-risk population for HIV infection. *Cultural Diversity and Ethnic Minority Psychology, 25*(1), 104.

Pleck J. H., Sonenstein, F. L., & Ku, L. C. (1993). Masculinity ideology: Its impact on adolescent males' heterosexual relationships. *Journal of Social Issues, 49*, 11–29.

Sikkema, K. J., Wagner, L. I., & Bogart, L. M. (2000). Gender and cultural factors in the prevention of HIV infection among women. In M. R. Eisler & M. Hersen (Eds.), *Handbook of gender, culture and health* (pp. 299–319). Mahwah: Lawrence Erlbaum Associates.

Stackman, V. R., Reviere, R., & Medley, B. C. (2016). Attitudes toward marriage, partner availability, and interracial dating among Black college students from Historically Black and predominately White institutions. *Journal of Black Studies, 47*(2), 169–192.

Strayhorn, T. L., & Tillman-Kelly, D. L. (2013). Queering masculinity: Manhood and Black gay men in college. *Spectrum: A Journal on Black Men, 1*(2), 83–110.

Stokes, L. R., & Brody, L. R. (2019). Self-Silencing, but not sexual relationship power associated with condom use for Black college-aged women. *Behavioral Sciences, 9*(2), 13.

Sutton, M. Y., Hardnett, F. P., Wright, P., Wahi, S., Pathak, S., Warren-Jeanpiere, L., & Jones, S. (2011). HIV/AIDS knowledge scores and perceptions of risk among African American students attending historically black colleges and universities. *Public Health Reports, 126*(5), 653–663.

The Opportunity Agenda (2011). Media representations and impact on the lives of Black men and boys. Retrieved from: https://www.opportunityagenda.org/explore/resources-publications/social-science-literature-review

Thomas, P. E., Voetsch, A. C., Song, B., Calloway, D., Goode, C., Mundey, L., Nobles, J....& Heffelfinger, J. D. (2008). HIV risk behaviors and testing history in historically Black college and university settings. *Public Health Reports, 123*, 115–125. 10.1177/00333549081230S314

Thomas, T. L., Yarandi, H. N., Dalmida, S. G., Frados, A., & Klienert, K. (2015). Cross-cultural differences and sexual risk behavior of emerging adults. *Journal of Transcultural Nursing, 26*(1), 64–72. 10.1177%2F104365 9614524791

Treadwell, H. M., Braithwaite, R. L., Braithwaite, K., Oliver, D., & Holliday, R. (2009). Leadership development for health researchers at historically Black colleges and universities. *American Journal of Public Health, 99*(S1), S53–S57.

Uecker, J. E., & Regnerus, M. D. (2010). Bare market: Campus sex ratios, romantic relationships, and sexual behavior. *The Sociological Quarterly, 51*, 408–435. 10.1111/j.1533-8525.2010.01177.x

Vandewater, E. A., Rideout, V. J., Wartella, E. A., Huang, X., Lee, J. H., & Shim, M. S. (2007). Digital childhood: electronic media and technology use among infants, toddlers, and preschoolers. *Pediatrics, 119*(5), e1006–e1015.

Wade, J. C. (2009). Traditional masculinity and African American men's health-related attitudes and behaviors. *American Journal of Men's Health, 3*(2), 165–172.

Winfield, E. B., & Whaley, A. L. (2005). Relationship status, psychological orientation, and sexual risk taking in a heterosexual African college sample. *Journal of Black Psychology, 31*, 189–204. 10.1177/0095798405274719

Wingood, G. M., & DiClemente, R. J. (1997). The effects of an abusive primary partner on the condom use and sexual negotiation practices of African American women. *American Journal of Public Health, 87*, 1016–1018.

Wingood, G. M., & DiClemente, R. J. (2006). Enhancing adoption of evidence–based HIV interventions: promotion of a suite of HIV prevention interventions for African American women. *AIDS Education & Prevention, 18*(supp), 161–170.

Wright, C. L., & Craske, M. (2015). Music's influence on risky sexual behaviors: Examining the cultivation theory. *Media Psychology Review, 9*(1). http://mprcenter.org/review/musics-influence-on-risky-sexual-behaviors-examining-the-cultivation-theory/

Wyatt, G. E. (2009). Enhancing cultural and contextual intervention strategies to reduce HIV/AIDS among African Americans. *American Journal of Public Health, 99*(11), 1941–1945.

Yarber, W. L., & Sayad, B. W. (2018). *Human Sexuality: Diversity in Contemporary America (10th edition)*. New York: McGraw Hill.

Younge, S. N., Boyer, C. B., Geter, A., Barker, J. C., & Corneille, M. (2014). An exploration of the sexual behaviors of emerging adult men attending a historically Black College/University. *Journal of Black Sexuality and Relationships, 1*(1), 65.

Younge, S. N., Smith, D., Young, L., Cole, D., Reynolds, L., Dixon, R.,... & Buchanan, P. N. (2007). Intersection between race, gender, and sexual risk: Implications for STI/HIV on HBCU campuses. *Challenge Online, 13*(2), 37–60.

Younge, S. N., Wade, B. H., Geter, A., Holliday, R. C., & Trawick, C. (2018). Condom attitudes and condom use among first year college men attending a historically Black institution. *American Journal of Health Studies, 33*(2), 80–88.

7   Violence and Sexual Health: A Culture of Silence?

Violence is a public health issue. Violence is a social justice issue. Violence is an HBCU issue. Because HBCUs are seen as microcosms of the larger Black community, there should be no surprise that any challenges in the broader community are also seen in the university setting. All college campuses must contend with sexual violence, which is an umbrella term that refers to crimes such as sexual assault, rape, intimate partner violence (IPV), cyberviolence, sexual harassment, and stalking (CDC, 2016). Experiencing a sexual assault (defined as any sexual act(s) committed against another person without their consent) can contribute to acute and chronic physical, emotional, and mental health consequences such as anxiety, including post-traumatic stress disorder (PTSD), depression, alcohol and substance abuse, and more (CDC, 2016; Lindquist et al., 2016). Consequences related directly to academia may include dropping classes (or out of the university), failing courses, transferring to another school, or ceasing attendance.

The national statistics for reported sexual violence are readily available, and the literature on sexual assault of college women is substantial. Nevertheless, there are very few studies focusing on Black college students (Lindquist et al., 2013) and even fewer concentrate on Black students at HBCUs. In the late 2000s, The National Institute of Justice funded RTI International to conduct the HBCU Campus Sexual Assault (HBCU-CSA) Study and document the prevalence of sexual assault, along with various factors (personal, behavioral, and contextual), and consequences related to the assault. Ten years ago, Krebs et al. (2011) published the results of this study – a cross-sectional survey of 3,951 undergraduate women (94.2% identified as Black) at four HBCUs. Within the sample, 86.31% of the students were between the ages of 18 and 24, 94.62% identified as heterosexual, and 43.92% were either in their freshman or sophomore year of school. Results indicated:

DOI: 10.4324/9781003180944-7

- 14.2% experienced an attempted or completed sexual assault since entering college
- 4.8% of the completed sexual assaults involved physical force

  - 38% of the physically forced assaults were by a dating partner, spouse, or previous partner
  - 37% of the physically forced assaults were by a classmate or fellow student

- 6.2% of the completed sexual assaults were while the person was incapacitated

  - 35% of the assaults while incapacitated were by a classmate or fellow student
  - 29% of the assaults while incapacitated were by an acquaintance
  - 26% of the assaults while incapacitated were by a 'friend'

- 41.9% of the assaults included alcohol or substance use

  - 5% of the assaults which included alcohol or substance use included a drug given without knowledge or consent

An interesting, but not statistically significant, finding from this study was that the largest percentage of sexual assaults took place in October, November, and then March. Most HBCU Homecomings are in October or November, and they are fraught with parties and events. These events often take place over a 1-week period and include university-sponsored concerts, Step Shows, parties, 'Yard Fest,' and alumni events. There are also events that take place off campus that are sponsored by community members and groups. March is the month in which Spring Break takes place in higher education. Students gear up to leave campus and head back home or on vacation with family and/or friends. During this time of year, one only needs to turn on the television or look at social media to see college students partying all over the globe. In anticipation of Homecoming and Spring Break events, an opportune time is presented to ramp up the discussions about drinking, substance use, safety, sexual activity, and consent.

Overall, CSA is underreported to law enforcement, and Black college women are significantly less likely to report an assault while incapacitated than White students (Krebs et al., 2011; Lindquist et al., 2013). Some reasons not to report an assault noted in both the Krebs et al. and Lindquist et al. studies include embarrassment, not wanting anyone to know, being afraid of retaliation, not knowing where or how to report, trust of university faculty and staff, and circumstances surrounding the assault and whether they will be believed. Krebs et al. found that 69.5% of the participants *strongly agreed* or *agreed* that they would not report to law enforcement because of the belief they would be treated poorly by police, lawyers, or other parts of the justice system. That percentage is not surprising, given the tense history between young Black individuals and law enforcement. However, it was not clear whether 'law enforcement' was referring to on-campus police or from the local police department. Students *may* have a better relationship with on-campus police than with those offsite.

As seen in the Krebs et al., study, most women experiencing CSA know the perpetrator as they were either a classmate, a romantic or sexual partner, or acquaintance. This, in the eyes of some survivors, brings about discussion regarding the legitimacy of the assault. Can you be raped by someone you regularly have sexual intercourse with? What if there are no visible injuries or it did not involve weapons? Palmer and St. Vil (2018) mention that survivors are more likely to report if they believe it is a 'real' rape, which means it is perpetrated by a stranger who uses a weapon and results in visible injuries. However, those factors are not common on college campuses. In fact, it is usually the opposite. More attention needs to be given to an unspoken culture of silence in some spaces. This silence can be around the actual assault and/or steeped in the stereotypes that Black women are hypersexual or 'rachet,' and that they should not tell 'outside' people their business and remain strong (i.e., Strong Black Woman). However, four out of five women (89.5%) *strongly agreed* or *agreed* that they would not report because they did not want to get the person in trouble. There is also a culture of silence based on who is the accused perpetrator (Tillman et al., 2010). There is a high likelihood, based on statistics, that the perpetrator was known to the survivor. Therefore, the decision to 'not get them in trouble' is made based on known characteristics, and perhaps contextual issues that require more exploration.

Although students may not report to law enforcement, students are likely to tell someone about the assault. Students may tell their friends, family members, the Resident Advisor in the dormitory, or even a faculty or staff member. I recall a situation with a student who reported a sexual assault by a member of the university football team. The alleged perpetrator was also an active member of a fraternal organization on campus. When the student sought assistance, she was met with multiple barriers that included being asked to recant the story multiple times, being asked "why were you there that late?" in an interview, and having her confidentiality breached.

There is still a substantial gap in the empirical literature about sexual violence on HBCUs campuses. More recently, Collington et al. (2019) conducted a study examining the prevalence, correlates, and outcomes of sexual assault at an HBCU. Of the 264 participants (71% female), 20.6% reported experiencing a sexual assault since coming to college. This percentage was higher than those reporting in the Krebs et al. study. Of those who reported experiencing a sexual assault since starting college, a large percentage of the survivor's used alcohol or other substances (20.7% and 96.7%, respectively) and so did their perpetrators (44.8% and 83.3%, respectively). Anxiety was the highest reported outcome from the sexual assault (70.4%) with 22.2% seeking medical treatment and 25.9% seeking counseling services.

One factor that may affect a person's risk for incapacitated sexual assault is whether a third party is willing to intervene, known as a bystander. Brown et al. (2014) investigated peer norms and bystander behavior among 232 college students (36% Black) at a southern PWI. Black students, both men and women, reported high bystander behavior when they believed their peers supported the behavior. What this demonstrates is the importance of peer and campus norms to students. This presents an opportunity to strategize ways to promote norms around disclosure, reporting, and intervening on campus. Bystander interventions are seen as an 'ecological approach to prevention' (McMahon & Banyard, 2012) because it supports a shared responsibility for action within the community, or in this case the campus community. Training students to identify potentially harmful situations and how to intervene and/or report them can be extremely beneficial for the campus but should be undertaken with great caution. Realistically, one must keep in mind that the bystander may also undergo some pushback from their peers for their actions and may initially be reluctant to intervene. The campus cultural dynamics, along with the personal dynamics of the parties involved, play a role in whether students decide to intervene. The goal is to empower students with the tools to report harmful behaviors and challenge a campus culture that punishes those who do report.

Sexual violence is increasing on campuses and has been highlighted in recent media on HBCU campuses. In an op-ed written for Teen Vogue, Clarissa Brooks (senior at the time, 2017) discusses what she calls the 'cultural complexities of HBCUs' and how it is related to sexual assault and violence (Brooks, 2017). Brooks outlines the time spent at Spelman College and how in 2006, the issue of sexual violence at Spelman and neighboring Morehouse College was brought to the public eye. During that time, Spelman students accused Morehouse students of sexual assault and since that time other accusations were made between students at both campuses. Laura Rahman, a Spelman graduate, and filmmaker created a short documentary in 2008 that explored sexual assault on the campuses of Spelman and Morehouse. The film, *Broken Social Contracts*, questioned what was perceived to be the complicity of Black leaders in power as it related to sexual violence. Various hashtags such as #*WeKnowWhatYouDid*, #*SilenceisViolence*, and a Twitter account @rapedatspelman gave students a voice. In 2015, both campuses were part of a list of over 100 institutions investigated for Title IX violations. Title IX is a Federal civil rights law that states *"No person in the United States shall, on the basis of sex, be excluded from participation in, be denied the benefits of, or be subjected to discrimination under any education program or activity receiving federal financial assistance"*(US Department of Education, 2021). Title IX covers education programs and activities within any school that receives any Federal funding. Under Title IX, discrimination based on sex can include sexual assault, violence, battery, harassment, and coercion.

Other HBCUs investigated for Title IX violations include Hampton University, Howard University, Morgan State University, and Prairie View A&M University. There have been student protests at some of these, and other HBCUs to draw attention to what students believe is a lack of appropriate response to sexual misconduct issues on campus. North Carolina A&T State University experienced some public outcry after a former cheerleader took to social media with her sexual assault. The former cheerleader was a freshman at the time she indicated the rape took place. She noted that the coaching staff was informed, but according to the student, their response was not sufficient. After an investigation concluded that there were Title IX violations, the Cheerleading squad was benched, and the coaches subsequently resigned. In 2019, the university updated its Title IX reporting policies and procedures. Referring to politics of respectability discussed in Chapter 1, the idea of respectability leaves little room for students speaking up and potentially 'sullying' the name and reputation of the university. There was backlash for some of the students who went public either with their experiences or those who supported others' experiences on campus. Additionally, if one claims multiple marginalized identities, the repercussions of reporting incidents and/or someone can be swift, harsh, and life-altering. Some students believe the costs of reporting and potentially being identified (lack of confidentiality) does not outweigh the benefits of having the perpetrator brought to justice (if that is the case).

Although the Collington et al. study included men, the highest reported rates of sexual assault on campuses are among women. As one reads this it should be obvious that there is a huge gap as it relates to Black men as survivors of sexual assault and violence. Sexual violence against emerging adult men is an underreported, yet significant problem that has been neglected in published literature. While the available statistics show that the percentage of men assaulted is significantly lower than women (Curry, 2019), it is common knowledge that men do not report sexual violence at the same rate as women. Some of the same challenges women have with reporting sexual violence (e.g., guilt, shame, embarrassment) men also have, coupled with a society that questions their sexuality, manhood, and physical and/or mental strength if they identify as a survivor.

In 2017, actor Terry Crews publicly announced on Twitter that in 2016 he was sexually assaulted by a high-level Hollywood executive at a party. Crews, a former player in the National Football League, was mocked by several high-profile entertainers on social media. Many of those who mocked, made fun, or made light of the situation were other Black men. In contrast, rapper, and actor Common revealed in 2019 that he was sexually abused as a child and received an outpouring of support on social media. He was a guest on *The Red Table Talk*, a show focused on frank discussion about important topics lead by actress Jada Pinkett Smith. During the segment, he talked about the impact the abuse had on his life and how he was not aware of the lasting trauma until he decided to seek psychological assistance. The difference between the two situations was stark. Perhaps it was the belief that since Common was a child, he could not protect himself and therefore should not be 'blamed' in this situation. On the opposite end of the perspective was that a strong, healthy man (Crews) should have never been a victim of a sexual assault ... and not at the hands of another man. He was blamed for the assault and ridiculed for not taking physical action against the perpetrator. This is a dangerous and slippery slope to travel down because there is an underlying value judgment about who is 'seen,' who is worthy of support, and who is expendable. Curry (2019) talks about how some researchers and scholars outright reject statistical data indicating that Black men are victims of sexual violence and assault at rates comparable to women. The gendered racism (Essed, 1991) experienced helps to explain why Black men are reluctant to disclose experiences of sexual violence. Gendered racism is a form of oppression experienced because of the intersection of race and gender and can help to explain why Black men who report sexual violence are not often taken seriously, and why this perspective reinforces the idea that only women can be victims or survivors.

Disclosure, with proper support, can be the difference in short- and long-term outcomes for survivors. In thinking about educational institutions, what system(s) are in place to support disclosure? Who are over these systems, and how qualified are they to support the students through the process? At a minimum, universities should be discussing sexual violence and providing, in writing, the protocol and names of the responsible individuals (and their administrative offices) to all students and their families. The protocol should be clear about what is confidential and what is not confidential, the flowchart for the procedure to report and to whom, the timeline for a response and appropriate action after the report, and what services are available to the survivor and the accused during this process.

To adequately address sexual violence on HBCU campuses, a 'one size cannot fit all' approach must be abandoned. Additionally, relying only on Title IX mandates to address the issue is not sufficient. Title IX Coordinators are required personnel at educational institutions receiving federal financial assistance and function to ensure situations comply with Title IX law. Many of these coordinators will need additional training to further strengthen their capacity to focus on the issues related to their responsibilities. Although many HBCUs already utilize culturally specific prevention and intervention approaches, more are needed. HBCUs need more counseling and wellness staff and advocates who are dedicated to addressing all types of violence on campus.

Finally, this may be an unpopular opinion but as a psychologist and as someone very much invested in uplifting the Black community, it would be great to see more resources allocated for perpetrators that are not wholly focused on retributive justice. This is not to absolve any perpetrator for their actions, it is however to invite discussion and action around rehabilitation of person – including perspective, attitudes, and actions. Violence is a learned, cultural phenomenon. Individuals grow up seeing, hearing about, and experiencing all types of violence in a multitude of ways. Through racial and gendered socialization, beliefs and behaviors are taught. Some imitate the negative behaviors and others do not. Some receive negative and harsh consequences for their actions, others are heralded and/or receive a slap on the hand. Either way, one of the goals is to get students to a place where they understand healthy interpersonal interactions which include consent and respect. Healing is also a goal. Violence is a public health issue. Violence is a social justice issue. Violence is an HBCU issue.

References

Brooks, C. (2017, December 21). *How HBCUs can make it hard for sexual assault survivors to speak up.* Teen Vogue. Retrieved from: https://www. teenvogue.com/story/hbcus-and-sexual-assault-op-ed

Brown, A. L., Banyard, V. L., & Moynihan, M. M. (2014). College students as helpful bystanders against sexual violence: Gender, race, and year in college moderate the impact of perceived peer norms. *Psychology of Women Quarterly, 38*(3), 350–362.

Centers for Disease Control and Prevention, National Center for Injury Prevention and Control, Division of Violence Prevention. (2016). *Sexual violence: Definitions.* Retrieved from https://www.cdc.gov/violenceprevention/ sexualviolence/definitions.html

Collington, D., Carter, M., Tolliver, A., & Turner-Musa, J. (2019). Sexual assault among college students attending a historically Black college/university. *American Journal of Undergraduate Research, 15*(4), 37.

Curry, T. J. (2019). Expendables for whom: Terry Crews and the erasure of Black male victims of sexual assault and rape. *Women's Studies in Communication, 42*(3), 287–307.

Essed, P. (1991). *Understanding everyday racism: An interdisciplinary theory* (Vol. 2). Sage.

Krebs, C. P., Lindquist, C. H., & Barrick, K. (2011). *The Historically Black College and University Campus Sexual Assault (HBCUCSA) Study* (Report No. 233614). Washington, D.C.: National Crime Justice Reference Service.

Lindquist, C. H., Crosby, C. M., Barrick, K., Krebs, C. P., & Settles-Reaves, B. (2016). Disclosure of sexual assault experiences among undergraduate women at historically Black colleges and universities (HBCUs). *Journal of American College Health, 64*(6), 469–480. 10.1080/07448481.2016.1181635

McMahon, S., & Banyard, V. L. (2012). When can I help? A conceptual framework for the prevention of sexual violence through bystander intervention. *Trauma, Violence, & Abuse, 13*(1), 3–14.

Palmer, J. E., & St. Vil, N. M. (2018). Sexual assault disclosure by college women at Historically Black Colleges and Universities and Predominantly White Institutions. *NASPA Journal About Women in Higher Education, 11*(1), 33–55.

Tillman, S., Bryant-Davis, T., Smith, K., & Marks, A. (2010). Shattering silence: Exploring barriers to disclosure for African American sexual assault survivors. *Trauma, Violence, & Abuse, 11*(2), 59–70.

U.S. Department of Education, Office for Civil Rights (2021). *Title IX and Sex Discrimination.* Retrieved from: https://www2.ed.gov/about/offices/list/ocr/ docs/tix_dis.html

8 Culturally Responsive Approaches to Sexual Health

Many researchers would advocate that culturally responsive approaches to sexual health prevention and intervention programming should be based on theoretical foundations. Theory-driven research is a useful tool in facilitating the understanding, prediction, and modification of beliefs, values, and behaviors associated with sexual health and sexual health outcomes. Theories have informed the extant sexual health literature in several ways including the increase of knowledge of the behavior change processes and constructs important to target in these processes. Although empirical studies utilizing theories of behavior change are available, empirical support for models applied to sexual behavior has been limited (Logan et al., 2002) except for HIV prevention and intervention. With the disparate rates and increasing incidence and prevalence of poorer sexual health outcomes among young Black college-aged individuals, the need to look beyond conventional knowledge of behavior change is critical. Some of the models and theories published have been developed and researched while utilizing a White, middle-class population yet their translation into successful prevention and intervention models with other populations has been met with mixed results.

Individual Level Frameworks

Early health behavior prevention frameworks (e.g., theory of reasoned action, theory of planned behavior, health belief model) posited that individuals who recognize that their behavior places them at risk for a disease or illness are more likely to adopt less risky behaviors than those who do not (Amaro, 1995; Kowalewski et al., 997). These first-generation theories laid the groundwork for future theories and interventions by examining variables such as perceived susceptibility, perceived severity, attitudes, beliefs, intentions, behavioral control,

DOI: 10.4324/9781003180944-8

and social norms. Each of these theories provide a unique understanding of the processes involved in changing risk behaviors associated with sexual health, particularly around reproductive health, and STI/HIV prevention. Sexual health promotion and interventions using these traditional health theories have shown some success, but they have received significant criticism regarding their applicability to minoritized populations, such as the Black community. Fisher and Fisher (2000) note many of the methodological weaknesses in the operationalization of some of these earlier theories. For example, the health belief model (HBM) is a commonly used model in STI/HIV prevention research and interventions, yet the relationships between some of the variables such as perceived risk and perceived vulnerability were thought to be nonspecific and hard to conceptualize (Fisher et al., 1994). The creators of the HBM (Rosenstock, 1974) have also acknowledged this weakness and as a result the HBM often is used in union with other models and theories.

Reese et al. (2020) used the HBM as the theoretical foundation to investigate what elements, according to the participants, impacted their sexual health and sexual behaviors. The qualitative study was conducted with 35 Black males at an HBCU through focus groups and one-on-one interviews. The study used the components of the HBM (perceived benefits, barriers, severity, and cues to action) to provide pilot data for sexual health programming and interventions. The findings indicated that the perceived benefits of safer (or perhaps healthier) sexual behavior were outweighed by the perceived severity, barriers, and cues to action. When thinking about developing culturally responsive approaches with emerging adults at HBCUs, it is important to understand from an emic perspective what is important to them, what are their identified barriers, and what are ways to alleviate these barriers. Research on Black males in college is lacking and research on those attending HBCUs is pretty much nonexistent. However, given the disproportionate rates of STIs and HIV for males in this age range (18–24 years), it is vital to comprehend what influences their sexual decision-making and behavior to reduce health disparities experienced by them. The participants in the Reese et al. study spoke about feeling as though there were expectations of engagement in risky sexual behavior that served as a deterrent for consistent safer sex practices. They were 'expected' to engage in risky behavior by their role as 'men' and the expectations that are associated with men. The perceived severity of the consequences of risky sexual behavior was not thought to be immediate and therefore they believed their health was not at risk. This was especially true of the participants who had sexual intercourse with women who disclosed they were using a hormonal birth control method.

The risk of an unplanned pregnancy was the immediate concern and therefore it went away with the disclosure. Although this was not identified in this study, there is a belief among many students that the severity of STIs, particularly the bacterial ones (e.g., chlamydia, gonorrhea), are not severe and can be cured quickly. However, there still appears to be a generalized lack of concern about viral STIs, including herpes and HIV, and the possibility of infection does not seem to be at the forefront of their minds. The element that crossed all influences of sexual health behaviors for the participants was the declaration of being a 'man.' The gendered and racial stereotypes and ideas they are exposed to regarding masculinity and manhood influenced the types of sexual behaviors they undertook. Additionally, participants spoke about not having condoms as a deterrent to safer sex behavior. This should bring up conversations about what services are offered to students on campus, and their associated costs.

The assumption that behaviors are voluntary and fully within an individual's control does not easily accommodate the larger social and cultural contexts in which risk behaviors occur in dealing with sexual risk behavior for young Black people. As a result, more recent research has examined what could be considered second-generation frameworks. These were developed based on individual psychosocial and cognitive approaches that educate individuals in practical skills to reduce their risk for poor sexual health outcomes such as unplanned pregnancies, STIs, and HIV (Kalichman & Hospers, 1997). These models (e.g., social cognitive theory, self-determination theory) used many of the same constructs as the first-generation theories such as self-efficacy, expectancies, intentions, motivation, and perceived vulnerability as playing important roles in prevention. Jenkins et al. (2020) used social cognitive theory (Bandura, 1986) as the theoretical foundation for a study with Black college students at an HBCU in the south. The social cognitive theory (SCT) posits that learning occurs in a dynamic context and those past experiences influence expectancies for behavior. The 282 participants (66.3% female) took a survey investigating their alcohol consumption, self-efficacy, alcohol expectancy, and their perceived control (related to drinking). Findings indicate that positive expectancies about alcohol consumption were significantly related to more drinking. In other words, if students perceived positive benefits from drinking, they were more likely to drink and to drink more than those who did not anticipate benefits from drinking. These benefits may include self-soothing, anxiety and/or stress reduction, increased socialization, and possibly as a coping mechanism for negative emotions such as loneliness (Jenkins et al., 2020). Research shows us a significant positive correlation between alcohol consumption and sexual risk behavior, and alcohol consumption and sexual violence. The use of this theoretical framework can assist with the creation of culturally responsive approaches to alcohol, and to some degree substance use, prevention, and intervention programming on HBCU campuses by focusing on open and honest conversations about the potentially negative effects of alcohol and substance use.

Social and Cultural Level Frameworks

Omitted in individual-level approaches are considerations (and integrations) of cultural and social factors (e.g., poverty, values, and practices of a specific group), structural factors, and situational factors that affect sexuality and sexual behaviors. In addition, many of the earlier models assume that people are quite reasonable, make systematic use of information, sexual behaviors and encounters are controlled completely by the individual, and that these encounters are always initiated under the individual's control (Amaro, 1995; Bruhin, 2003). The application of these theories and models often fails to include structural and situational variables that are common in sexual relationships such as unequal power dynamics, gender roles, and the need for intimacy that put individuals at risk.

Social science researchers have come to realize that because complex health behaviors such as sex take place in a cultural milieu, sociocultural factors surrounding the individual must be considered in designing prevention interventions. Theories from a contextual perspective consider the importance of external economic and racial/ethnic discriminatory factors, and include the language, customs, rituals, beliefs, values, thoughts, communication, and actions that are appropriate for the individuals under study. Rather than singularly focus on psychological processes as the basis for sexual behavior, the focus on behavior change in these models tends to be on social norms, relationships, and gender imbalances that create the meaning and determinants of behavior and behavior change. In examining the various psychosocial and sociocultural influences on sexual health for young Black college students, it seems natural that they would be included in the theories, models, and frameworks used with this population.

Theory of Gender and Power

Many researchers have suggested the use of gender-sensitive theoretical frameworks to provide a more complete understanding of the decision to engage in HIV preventative behaviors (Cochran & Mays,

1993; Wingood & DiClemente, 1998; Worth, 1990). One such framework, the theory of gender and power (TGP; Connell, 1987) is a social structural theory that builds upon the variables in these earlier models that have proven successful in examining and creating behavior change. Unlike many individual-level frameworks which are essentially gender-blind, the TGP addresses the wider social and environmental issues surrounding gender dynamics, such as distribution of power and authority, affective influences, and gender-specific norms within heterosexual relationships. The TGP has been applied to HIV prevention and intervention studies with Black women by Wingood and DiClemente (2000). The TGP suggests that gender inequality manifests itself in power imbalances which may affect an individual's ability to navigate through social and sexual environments. The imbalances can account for a person's willingness to adopt and maintain sexual risk reduction strategies within heterosexual relationship, perceptions of power, commitment to the relationship, and role in the relationship (Prather et al., 2006). According to the theory, three major structures characterize the gendered relationships between men and women: the sexual division of labor, the sexual division of power, and the structure of cathexis. These three overlapping but distinct structures are thought to help explain the culturally bound social roles assumed by men and women. The three structures are inextricably linked and cannot be independent from one another (Connell, 1987).

Francis et al. (2018) evaluated the efficacy of a 3-month HIV prevention condom distribution and health communication intervention for Black women attending an all-female HBCU in North Carolina. Free condoms, via dispensers, were provided with culturally relevant messaging on the dispensers. The CDC endorses condom distribution projects and programs as a cost-effective structural intervention to provide resources needed to prevent the acquisition and transmission of STIs, including HIV. TGP served as one of the theoretical frameworks used to create the health messaging content on the dispensers as it posits that negative beliefs about women carrying condoms may put them at greater risk for unplanned pregnancies, STIs, and HIV by creating taboos about what is acceptable in expression of sexuality (DiClemente & Wingood, 2000). Changing the environment along with positive culturally relevant messaging is one way to counteract negative attitudes, beliefs, and stereotypes about safer sex practices. Results of the intervention indicated that more than 50% of those students who saw the dispensers used them to access the condoms. While condom availability and accessibility significantly increased after the intervention, condom use declined over time. The authors believed that relationship status and/or type of relationship influenced the decision to stop using condoms. Of course, this is not unusual as perceived relationship status (including length of time knowing the partner and affection felt for the partner) is related to inconsistent and condom non-use. As a final note on TGP, to the author's knowledge, the TGP has not been utilized with a comparative population of men to see if the benefits that are afforded them in society, based on gender, have an opposite effect on their sexual behavior. While gender affords men certain opportunities over women in the larger society, the social construct of race dictates a lower social status for Black men. Examining the nexus of gender, race, and its impact on sexual behavior provides an interesting and intriguing interpretation of the theory.

Sexual Scripting Theory

Sexual scripting theory (SST) can be used to understand the intersection between individual-level behaviors, rules and norms for sexual interactions, and the broader social structures (Fasula et al., 2014). SST provides a framework to explore and understand sexual conduct (e.g., decisions about sexual health, sexual behavior) (Gagnon & Simon, 1973; Simon & Gagnon, 2003). Sexual scripts are frameworks of meanings and behaviors built by cultural or social groups and transformed by persons to contextualize their (sexual) experiences. SST posits that an individual's sexual health and behavior are produced by three interacting scripts: cultural scenarios, interpersonal scripts, and intrapsychic scripts. Ideally, all three levels of sexual scripts influence all aspects of sexual health and behavior, including how one conceptualizes sexual health, who one has sex with, which activities should be done, and when and where these activities take place. The intersection of these three levels shape sexual health and behavior in a dynamic process (Hussen et al., 2012). Although scripts are likely to fluctuate due to developmental changes, it is important to examine these scripts among college students as this is a evolving period where sexual attitudes, expectations, and decisions about health and behavior are often established and carried into adulthood.

The author and a team of researchers have a paper currently under review that provides much-needed data on young Black men attending HBCUs and the influence of media and music on the construction and enactment of masculinities. The study used SST as the framework to explore the influence of popular figures and technology on Black masculinities and subsequent sexual behavior. A sample of 23 male and female students (between the ages of 18 and 24 years) from two HBCUs participated in one of six focus groups held on their respective campuses. Following analysis of the focus group data, the research team found three themes that speak to the variations and situational construction, enactment, and/or performance of masculinities in this generation (Generation Z) that are informed by this immersion in media and music. First, the fluidity of Black male representation in the media was discussed at length by participants. Due to the wide access smartphones provide, there were multiple representations and portrayals of Black male figures that were mentioned as influencing their creation and enactment of sexual scripts. For example, one of the participants mentioned DJ Khaled and how he once indicated that as the provider in the household, there are certain sexual activities that do not have to be reciprocated, such as oral sex. This intrapsychic script described and discussed by the participants focused on personal conceptions of sexuality and how positionality impacts these schemas and scripts. Secondly, the theme of social media realities versus expectations was discussed as a cultural script represented by stereotypical masculine gender presentation online. Young men who identified as gay or bisexual talked about how 'more' masculine images garner more 'likes' from other men, and those images deemed to be 'more' feminine do not garner the same type of attention. Therefore, young men learn that a certain gender expression and presentation is more acceptable. Within this same theme, young women in the focus groups talked about the pressure of using social media filters (i.e., to enhance a picture) to appear more attractive, to have a lighter skin tone, or to appear slimmer for prospective partners. Finally, the participants discussed how pornography informed the performance and enactment of masculinities through their sexual behavior, beginning in their youth. Irrespective of the sexual orientation or age of the male participant, all described how watching pornography during adolescence shaped their (inaccurate) expectations of sexual behavior with partner(s), and their interpersonal interactions with potential romantic and/or sexual partners. An important note was that young men who identified as gay or bisexual mentioned that pornography played a significant role in learning more about their sexual identities and interests as they developed. There was a robust conversation about 'traditional' gender roles and expectations. As Hall et al. (2012) note, much of masculinity literature uses 'traditional' as a term synonymous with 'conservative;' however, based on the unique sociopolitical and sociosexual histories, this may not translate the same with young Black individuals. Black men and women may apply this term utilizing different operationalization and experiential understanding in describing and perceiving their masculinities. More culturally and ecologically appropriate research on the masculinities of young Black men in college is sorely needed.

Bridging the Gap

There have been numerous theories, models, and frameworks used in research that seeks to explain how young people receive, interpret, and utilize health information. Bridging the gap is operationally defined as the disjunction between theoretical perspective and attitudes and behaviors of the population. It cannot be overstated that knowledge or even skill alone cannot eliminate sexual health disparities for young Black college students. There should be a multi-dimensional and, in some instances, multi-pronged approach to examining individual, social, cultural, and contextual factors that influence overall sexual health and specifically sexual decision-making and sexual behavior.

HIV Prevention and Intervention

The decision to dedicate a separate section to HIV prevention and intervention for Black college students is based on the known risks that are associated with disproportionate prevalence and incidence rates. As reported elsewhere, young Black college-aged adults have disparate rates of STI and HIV infection. Given the latency period for HIV, it is quite possible that many of the incidence and prevalence rates seen for Black people in their mid to late 20s are a result of being infected during their college years. The author can think of no other infectious disease, in modern times, that has warranted the development of so many theory-based prevention and intervention programs. This is particularly true for Black individuals in the United States.

The HIV National Strategic Plan (2021–2025) details the roadmap for ending the HIV epidemic by 2030. The four goals of the most recent plan are to: 1) prevent new HIV infections; 2) improve HIV-related health outcomes of people with HIV; 3) reduce HIV-related disparities and health inequities; and 4) achieve integrated and coordinated efforts that address the HIV epidemic among all partners and stakeholders (United States Department of Health and Human Services [USDHHS], 2021). The HIV Plan prioritizes efforts to reduce the disparities and inequities, and improve outcomes for the following:

- Gay, bisexual, and other men who have sex with men, in particular Black, Latino, and American Indian/Alaska Native men;
- Black women;
- Transgender women;
- Youth aged 13–24 years; and
- People who inject drugs.

All the subpopulations mentioned above are part of the HBCU family. The role of HBCUs in HIV education and prevention continues to be an important one. A unique contribution of HBCUs to HIV prevention, compared with other educational institutions, is that they are largely grounded in a communal/collectivist approaches to student success. These approaches can work for HIV prevention by stressing the importance of accurately assessing and reducing risk as part of a family and broader communal imperative. Successful HIV interventions for young Black people can benefit from the inherent strength and communal perspectives of HBCUs.

As guided by the National HIV/AIDS Strategy for the United States, the CDC has a compendium of effective behavioral interventions (EBIs) that can be accessed, free of charge from its website (https://www.cdc.gov/ hiv/effective-interventions/index.html). There are several EBIs specifically tailored for young Black men and women, although most focus on community populations because of the immediate need to address the personal, social, cultural, and systemic factors that contribute to their increased risk and rates of infection and transmission. Some of these theoretically grounded interventions include:

- *d-up: Defend Yourself!* is an HIV prevention intervention for Black men who have sex with men (MSM) that promotes condom use as a social norm and assists Black MSM navigate risk-related racial and sexual bias.
- *Many Men, Many Voices (3MV)* is an HIV prevention intervention designed to increase condom use for Black MSM who may or may not identify themselves as gay/same-gender-loving.
- *Sister to Sister* is an STI/HIV prevention intervention (delivered during a routine medical visit) focused on enhancing Black women (ages 18 and older) knowledge, beliefs, confidence, and skills to reduce their risk.
- *SISTA (Sisters Informing Sisters on Topics about AIDS)* is an STI/ HIV prevention intervention designed to increase assertiveness, condom negotiations skills, and coping skills while promoting gender and ethnic pride and empowerment.

There have been some cultural adaptations of the above EBIs for other populations such as Black college students. Additionally, there has been an uptick on the development and testing of other HIV prevention interventions for Black emerging adults in college. However, not many focus on the social and cultural context of HBCUs. One promising intervention being developed and piloted with Black college students (both men and women) at HBCUs and other Minority-Serving Institutions (MSIs) in the South is the **Engag3 HIV Prevention Intervention** (Dyson, 2021). *Engag3* is an evidence-based intervention that was adapted from the CDC's Healthy Love intervention for Black women. It is a *sex positive*, brief, highly interactive, single session, 3.5-hour group-level intervention designed to decrease sexual risk behaviors. Specifically, it promotes safe sexual practices of Black college students across all ages. The culturally responsive prevention intervention is delivered by a lead Certified Healthy Love Prevention Intervention Facilitator, along with another Black Facilitator. The theoretical foundation of the intervention is guided by the **Integrated Model for Behavioral Prediction** to assess the intention to *engage* in a behavior and **Intersectionality Theory** that acknowledges the various intersecting identities that Black college students embody in addition to addressing the intersection between mental health and physical health, binge drinking, and perception of HIV risk. Results from the original pilot study revealed that a single session intervention that interactively *engaged* students showed promise for future implementation. Additionally, findings from the pilot study also revealed that brief, culturally relevant, empowerment-based prevention interventions that infuse pop culture and constantly engage participants are enough to sustain Black college students' attention and increase the likelihood that they would be motivated to change sexual risk behaviors.

In sum, the disproportionate number of HIV/AIDS cases among Black individuals, combined with the high levels of sexual experimentation and prevalence of STIs among young people, suggests that Black college students are at higher risk and should be a programmatic AND research priority. Despite the critical transition that these young people are making, few researchers have focused on students attending HBCUs. What is desperately needed is a better understanding of factors associated with Black college students' preventive and risky sexual decision-making and behavior. This will help guide the development of strategies and interventions to reduce the rate of STIs, including HIV, in this population, and advance the translation of culturally grounded research into effective practice. The last chapter provides some recommendations on how to achieve optimal sexual and reproductive health for Black college students at HBCUs.

References

Amaro, H. (1995). Love, sex, power: Considering women's realities in HIV prevention. *American Psychologist, 50,* 437–447.

Bandura, A. (1986). The explanatory and predictive scope of self-efficacy theory. *Journal of Social and Clinical Psychology, 4*(3), 359–373.

Bruhin, E. (2003). Power, communication and condom use: Patterns of HIV-relevant sexual risk management in heterosexual relationships. *AIDS Care, 15*(3), 389–401.

Cochran, S. D., & Mays, V. M. (1993). Applying social psychological models to predicting HIV-related sexual risk taking behaviors among African Americans. *Journal of Black Psychology, 19,* 142–154.

Connell, R. W. (1987). *Gender and power.* Stanford, CA: Stanford University Press.

DiClemente, R. J., & Wingood, G. M. (2000). Expanding the scope of HIV prevention for adolescents: Beyond individual-level interventions. *Journal of Adolescent Health, 26*(6), 377–378.

Fasula, A. M., Carry, M., & Miller, K. S. (2014). A multidimensional framework for the meanings of the sexual double standard and its application for the sexual health of young Black women in the US. *The Journal of Sex Research, 51*(2), 170–183.

Fisher, J. D., Fisher, W. A., Williams, S. S., & Malloy, T. E. (1994). Empirical tests of an information-motivation-behavioral skills model of AIDS-preventive behavior with gay men and heterosexual university students. *Health Psychology, 13*(3), 238.

Fisher, J. D., & Fisher, W. A. (2000). Theoretical approaches to individual-level change in HIV risk behavior. In *Handbook of HIV prevention* (pp. 3–55). Springer, Boston, MA.

Francis, D. B., Noar, S. M., Fortune, D. A., & Adimora, A. A. (2018). "Be straight up and so will he": Evaluation of a novel HIV prevention condom distribution and health communication intervention targeting young African American females. *AIDS Education and Prevention, 30*(2), 137–151.

Gagnon, J. H., & Simon, W. (1973). *Sexual conduct: The social sources of human sexuality.* Chicago: Aldine.

Hall, N. M., Morales, D. A., Coyne-Beasley, T. & St. Lawrence, J. (2012). Correlates of African American men's sexual schemas. *Sex Roles, 67*(11-12), 670–681. PMC3767847

Hussen, S. A., Bowleg, L., Sangaramoorthy, T., & Malebranche, D. J. (2012). Parents, peers and pornography: The influence of formative sexual scripts on adult HIV sexual risk behaviour among Black men in the USA. *Culture, Health & Sexuality, 14*(8), 863–877.

Jenkins, P. R., Hernandez, P. M., & Harris, C. A. (2020). African American college students' drinking behaviors and their relationship to self-efficacy and positive or negative expectancies regarding alcohol consumption. *Behavioral Sciences, 10*(10), 153.

Kalichman, S. C., & Hospers, H. J. (1997). Efficacy of behavioral-skills en-
hancement HIV risk-reduction interventions in community settings. *AIDS
(London, England)*, *11*, S191–S199.

Kowalewski, M. R., Henson, K. D., & Longshore, D. (1997). Rethinking
perceived risk and health behavior: A critical review of HIV prevention
research. *Health Education & Behavior*, *24*(3), 313–325.

Logan, T. K., Cole, J., & Leukefeld, C. (2002). Women, sex, and HIV: Social
and contextual factors, meta-analysis of published interventions, and implications for practice and research. *Psychological Bulletin*, *128*(6), 851.

Prather, C., Fuller, T. R., King, W., Brown, M., Moering, M., Little, S., et al.
(2006). Diffusing an HIV prevention intervention for African American
women: Integrating Afrocentric components into the SISTS diffusion
strategy. *AIDS Education and Prevention*, *18*, 149–160.

Reese, N., Mincey, K. D., & Felder, K. (2020). Understanding what influences
sexual health behaviors among Black males in college. *Journal of Black
Sexuality and Relationships*, *6*(3), 13–27.

Rosenstock, I. M. (1974). The health belief model and preventive health behavior. *Health Education Monographs*, *2*(4), 354–386.

Simon, W., & Gagnon, J. H. (2003). Sexual scripts: Origins, influences and
changes. *Qualitative Sociology*, *26*(4), 491–497.

U.S. Department of Health and Human Services (2021). *HIV National
Strategic Plan for the United States: A Roadmap to End the Epidemic
2021–2025*. Washington, DC.

Wingood, G. M., & DiClemente, R. J. (1998). Partner influences and gender-
related factors associated with noncondom use among young adult African
American women. *American Journal of Community Psychology*, *26*, 29–51.

Wingood, G. M., & DiClemente, R. J. (2000). Application of the theory of
gender and power to examine HIV-related exposures, risk factors, and effective interventions for women. Health education & behavior, *27*(5),
539–565.

Worth, D. (1990). Sexual decision making and AIDS: Why condom promotion among vulnerable women is likely to fail. *Studies of Family Planning*,
20, 297–307.

9 Sexual Health Promotion on HBCU Campuses

This final chapter focuses on recommendations to enhance positive sexual and reproductive health on HBCU campuses by increasing access to early prevention and treatment resources, and ways to support students through the critical transition into emerging adulthood.

Health promotion is defined as any planned combination of educational, political, regulatory, and organizational supports for actions and conditions of living conducive to the health of individuals, groups, or communities (Green & Kreuter, 1991). What does successful sexual health promotion policies and programs look like at HBCUs? What should be included?

Access and Acceptance

Sexual and reproductive health are critical to overall student development and requires more culturally relevant and responsive attention. HBCUs have a duty to promote and provide appropriate health services to its students. As institutions that are considered 'high touch,' HBCUs must provide access to sexual health information that is developmentally and culturally appropriate, medically accurate, incorporates activities that allow students to practice and enhance their skills, and is delivered by individuals who are non-judgmental and encourage healthy sexual development. These services would be designed to model acceptance of diverse identities, expressions, and sexual health needs. It cannot be stated enough that sexual health encompasses more than just sexuality and sexual behavior; however, most services provided for students on campus only focus on pregnancy and STI/HIV prevention. Students in the emerging adult developmental stage have a wide variety of sexual and reproductive health concerns and needs that can be addressed by universities who invest in something as simple as a campus needs assessment.

DOI: 10.4324/9781003180944-9

Sexuality, sexual health, and sexual behavior are all topics that may invoke feelings of discomfort from some faculty and staff; however, those who are charged with working with students to address these issues must be comfortable enough to guide students through the discovery, and in some instances, acceptance processes. While students are attending and matriculating through the university, they are developing various aspects of their identities, including their sexual one. If HBCU campuses are analogous to communities in which people are to live and thrive, they must provide the opportunities to do so, within the campus community. The creation of inclusive, safe, non-judgmental, and supportive sexual health education and services is critical. This is not to imply that many HBCUs do not already offer these services or serve students in this manner. It is, however, to acknowledge that even with what is currently offered, the sexual health outcomes of Black college students attending HBCUs are still markedly poorer than college students of other racial/ethnic groups. *Why?* Of course, there are a myriad of possible responses to the question, but the bottom line is that HBCUs need to ensure they are not stagnant on issues related to sexual health so that all students can thrive. Each university must be visibly invested in optimal sexual health promotion to the students. One of the recurring issues on many campuses is low utilization of services, particularly those related to sexual health. Some of the reasons may include student perceptions of confidentiality, limited services, and lack of cultural responsiveness. The goal is to have a thriving program that is designed to serve students in a manner that will promote, and sustain, positive sexual health. In a study with 119 Black women attending an HBCU, 85% indicated that their most common source of sexual health education was school, followed by home (74%), peers (66%), media (50%), and then all other sources (5%) (Francis et al., 2018). If the campus environment is one that students depend upon for knowledge and accurate information, there should be action on the part of the university. However, just because services are offered does not mean students will utilize them. So how can HBCUs ensure that the appropriate services are being offered and increase the chances that students are accessing them?

Culturally Responsive Programming

One strategy is to focus on cultural, contextual, and structural factors that influence and impact sexual health for young Black college students, first and foremost. The focus of HBCUs is on racial pride and uplift, character development, and leadership development. HBCUs provide an experience that promotes personal and professional growth, and part of this growth is optimal health and well-being. Black excellence is at the center of HBCUs, and any sexual health program must incorporate this perspective. Using an empowerment framework (see Opara et al., 2020) to acknowledge the historical and current social inequities that may serve as impediments but utilizing racial identity and pride as protective factors for action. Sexual health programs at HBCUs should highlight the strengths, resiliency, support, creativity that is indicative of Black culture. Services should be gender and culturally specific and focus on strengths-based and empowering prevention and intervention, not pathologizing the students or focusing solely on the adverse sexual health outcomes. It should focus on more than just preventing pregnancy and/or disease.

Another strategy is to make sure students feel valued and respected, irrespective of their identities and/or choices. Black students do not have the privilege to ignore race, racism, and sexism as it permeates through every aspect of their daily lives. Therefore, the conceptualizations of race, and identity must be considered when developing any successful, effective programming. What would be the purpose of having race-neutral services at universities designed to celebrate Blackness? Along with using an empowerment framework, focusing on prevention and intervention models that incorporate an Afrocentric approach can be beneficial for Black students. There is evidence that youth and young adults are more likely to participate in interventions that are culturally relevant (Metzger et al., 2013). As college students are engaged in a continuing developmental process, which includes racial and ethnic identity development, interventions that target the reduction of risky behaviors may have greater effect if they incorporate positive cultural affirmations while promoting a positive sense of self and cultural pride (Heads et al., 2017). Increasing one's positive views of their race and/or ethnicity is related to increased self-esteem and self-worth (Fisher et al., 2017). Therefore, the belief is that those who view themselves in higher regards and understand their connection with others like them may mediate engagement in behavior that can be damaging to them or their community.

Reimagining Sexual Health Promotion on HBCU Campuses

Based on available empirical research, the following are additional suggestions for sexual health promotion on HBCU campuses. This list is by no means exhaustive, but should be used to think about needs assessments and planning to serve and support our students:

Mandatory Classes/Trainings

Most universities have Freshman and Transfer Student orientations, or some type of class/program used to introduce incoming students to the overall structure of the university, the administrators, student services, and to each other. As more universities incorporate sessions about student conduct and behavior, it seems like a good fit to also include topics related to sexual health. This session must include information about Title IX but should go beyond the legal implications of the federal mandate. There must be clear expectations about student conduct, reporting, and consequences of sexual violence. These sessions and/or classes can provide a space for students to discuss views, concerns, and ask questions of trained facilitators who are comfortable leading the sessions. This information is so vital to the development and conduct of students on campus that it should be repeated regularly. The past few years showed academia that it can deliver quality education via digital technologies, and this modality should be considered for 'refresher' courses on topics. The importance of refresher courses is based in the fact that students are constantly evolving and often have different needs, questions, and concerns as they mature. All sexual health programming should account for these developmental changes. One of the courses recommended is an introductory course to sexual health and/or human sexuality.

- *Sexual Health 101.* As an HBCU professor who teaches Health Psychology and Psychology of Human Sexuality, I have noticed the lack of knowledge or the amount of misinformation that students have about their bodies, feelings, and behavior is always alarming. Much of the information they have is heavily skewed in the direction of sexual behavior, but less in the direction of equally important aspects of sexual health such as anatomy and physiology, cognition, and/or psychological influences on sexual health. This is supported by several researchers who have called for mandatory infusions of sexual health information across the curriculum at HBCUs (see Perkins et al., 2020; Francis et al., 2018).

Pregnancy and STI/HIV Prevention and Intervention Services

Pregnancy prevention is included with STI and HIV services because the same messaging about increasing safer sex behaviors to prevent STIs, including HIV can be used for preventing unplanned pregnancies.

Although the rates of unplanned pregnancies have steadily decreased among 18–24-year-old, the rates of STIs and HIV have not. Much of the decrease in pregnancy rates are due to the increase in hormonal contraceptives taken by women. Including the services together presents an opportunity to discuss what a significant portion of students are concerned about (pregnancy prevention) in an environment that also provides essential testing for STIs and HIV.

- *Gendered Services.* It is important to acknowledge and respond to the varying needs of those who identify across the gender spectrum. Research continuously indicates that gender identity is influential in how knowledge is processed, accepted, and implemented. Studies show that females, in general, have more accurate knowledge of sexual health issues than males. Additionally, females often have more positive attitudes toward condoms and condoms use than males. However, there is a dearth of information specifically tailored to those who do not identify as binary. As we consider gendered services, we must be cognizant that gender, gender identity, and gender expression do not necessarily include sexuality. Services are often inherently cisgendered and exclude gender nonconforming and transgendered students. Cisgender describes individuals whose assigned sex at birth is in alignment with their gender identity. Rubinsky and Cooke-Johnson (2017) noted that when adult women were asked which messages about sexual they wish they would have received, approximately 21% desired conversations that exposed them to diverse gender and sexual identities and for the information to be from a "less heteronormative, cisnormative and (cis)male-centric point of view" (p. 391).

- *HIV Counseling, Testing, and PrEP Services.* Many college health centers offer HIV counseling and testing, or they refer to the local health department. There are concerns with keeping the services onsite (e.g., confidentiality); however, it is possible to design an intake and testing system that protects the privacy rights of individuals. Many university counseling and wellness centers have systems in place to ensure the privacy of students receiving services is protected. What is missing with many universities, particularly HBCUs is PrEP. PrEP is pre-exposure prophylaxis, a daily medication that may prevent individuals at risk for HIV through sex or injection drug use from becoming infected. As noted by Okeke et al. (2021), PrEP use by college-aged students (18–24) is suboptimal, and less than 15% of young people who could benefit from PrEP received a prescription for it. Clinical trials indicate the PrEP, taken as prescribed, is 92–98% effective in preventing HIV among some of the highest risk populations (e.g., men who have sex with men, injection drug users). While this is not an endorsement of PrEP use, it is an acknowledgment of the role that HBCUs can play in reducing the acquisition and spread of HIV amongst its students. Okeke et al. assessed the feasibility and acceptability of PrEP on HBCU campuses by administering a survey to 210 students (75% women/89% heterosexual) at two HBCUs in North Carolina. The study asked students about PrEP awareness and acceptability. Most respondents (52%) were aware of PrEP and indicated they would consider taking it daily (58%); however, 73% felt that they were 'not at all at risk' for HIV. This previously stated challenge, students underestimating their risk for HIV, presents an enormous challenge to encouraging students to consider PrEP. Overall, PrEP use among young Black college-aged individuals is low, even among those at highest risk (Chandler et al., 2021). There are valid concerns regarding PrEP uptake that include the perception that it will undermine education and risk reduction efforts on campus and in the community. Additionally, there are questions and concerns about the long-term effects of use, and possible financial costs associated with its use. The Student Health Centers on campus can serve as an effective promotor of accurate information for students regarding PrEP so that they can make an informed choice for themselves. PrEP may be an option for those students who are not at a place of comfort in condom negotiation with partner(s) but would like to have some semblance of protection for sexual intercourse. Additionally, it may be an option for students who have not fully embraced, or reconciled, their identity and engage in behaviors that may not be in sync with how they personally or socially identity themselves.

LGBTQ+ Services

Many HBCUs are thought to embody politically and socially conservative ideals, irrespective of their designation as a private or public institution. Unfortunately, these conservative ideals are often associated with policies and exclusionary perspectives that are seen as 'unwelcoming' by some students (Mobley & Hall, 2020). Empirical literature focused on the sexual health needs, practices, and outcomes for Black college students who identify as gender non-conforming or transgendered are almost non-existent. Since representation matters, it is imperative to ensure that students know that they are not a 'distraction' because their identities and expressions are perhaps different from most students on campus. Sexual health is connected to one's identity and their overall positive psychological well-being. Having access to culturally relevant and responsive sexually health information is important for *all* students.

While a major focus at HBCUs is on racial and cultural pride, this should not be at the peril of other important identities. Scholars, practitioners, educators, and administrators must be conscious of heterosexual privilege in designing services. To be realistic, it is not possible to be everything to every student; however, there are bastions of data available on the sexual health needs of young people in the emerging adulthood stage. Collaborative efforts such as partnerships between the Office of Institutional Research, Student Health, and perhaps Student Affairs to conduct regular needs assessments on campus as a way of identifying overall, and specific needs of the student population is a simple, yet effective way of being inclusive and supportive. There is a pressing need to reimagine approaches that embrace and support aspects of a student's identity beyond race (Mobley & Johnson, 2019; Njoku et al., 2017). While this list is not exhaustive, here are some HBCUs that have prioritized supporting LGBTQ+ students by creating inclusive spaces:

Public HBCUs

- Virginia State University (Petersburg, Virginia) has gender neutral restrooms on campus
- North Carolina A&T State University (Greensboro, NC) recently opened a new student center in the Fall of 2018, includes gender neutral restroom
- Savannah State University (Savannah, Georgia) – gender neutral housing options
- Norfolk State University (Norfolk, Virginia) – gender neutral housing options
- North Carolina Central University (Durham, North Carolina) – gender neutral housing options
- Morgan State University (Baltimore, Maryland) – gender neutral housing options
- Bowie State University (Bowie, Maryland) – the first HBCU to launch an LGBTQ Health Center

Private HBCUs

- Johnson C. Smith University (Charlotte, North Carolina) – gender neutral housing options

- Howard University (Washington, D. C.) – gender neutral housing options

As mentioned repeatedly throughout the book, the developmental transition from high school to college presents opportunities and numerous challenges for emerging adults. However, the transition to a college campus exposes students to a variety of opportunities to engage in activities that could be considered high risk. The focus should be on normalizing discussions about sexual and reproductive health, and actively working toward instituting culturally responsive policies and approaches as a way of demonstrating respect for all persons.

To close the chapter, and book, here are five questions for consideration:

1 Does your university conduct an annual campus culture survey to assist with academic and administrative planning?

2 Are the policies and systems on your campus designed to support students with diverse gender, racial, and sexuality identities and expressions, or do they serve as an impediment for students? Are they rooted in politics of respectability?

3 Are the university-sponsored organizations, activities, and communications rooted in heteronormative language and practices? If yes, how might you begin the process of changing this?

4 Does the health and wellness services offered on campus use culturally responsive approaches to enhance the sexual and reproductive health choices and outcomes for students? If not, why?

5 Are there adequate resources allocated to serve the reproductive, sexual, and mental health needs for students on campus? If not, what are some strategies that can help facilitate a reallocation of funds and priorities?

References

Chandler, R., Guillaume, D., Tesema, N., Paul, S., Ross, H., & Hernandez, N. D. (2021). Social and environmental influences on sexual behaviors of college Black women: Within group diversity between HBCU vs. PWI experiences. *Journal of Racial and Ethnic Health Disparities*, 8(4), 852–862.

Fisher, S., Zapolski, T. C., Sheehan, C., & Barnes-Najor, J. (2017). Pathway of protection: Ethnic identity, self-esteem, and substance use among multiracial youth. *Addictive Behaviors*, 72, 27–32. 10.1016/j.addbeh.2017.03.003

Francis, D. B., Noar, S. M., Fortune, D. A., & Adimora, A. A. (2018). "Be straight up and so will he": Evaluation of a novel HIV prevention condom distribution and health communication intervention targeting young African American females. *AIDS Education and Prevention*, *30*(2), 137–151.

Green, L. W., & Kreuter, M. W. (1991). *Health education planning*. Mayfield Pub. Co.

Heads, A. M., Dickson, J. W., & Asby, A. T. (2017). Correlates of HIV risk-taking behaviors among African-American college students: HIV knowledge and ethnic identity. *Journal of Health Care for the Poor and Underserved*, *28*(2), 155–170.

Metzger, I., Cooper, S. M., Zarrett, N., & Flory, K. (2013). Culturally sensitive risk behavior prevention programs for African American adolescents: A systematic analysis. *Clinical Child and Family Psychology Review*, *16*(2), 187–212. 10.1007/s10567-013-0133-3

Mobley Jr, S. D., & Hall, L. (2020). (Re) Defining queer and trans* student retention and "success" at Historically Black Colleges and Universities. *Journal of College Student Retention: Research, Theory & Practice*, *21*(4), 497–519.

Mobley Jr, S. D., & Johnson, J. M. (2019). "No pumps allowed": The "problem" with gender expression and the Morehouse College "Appropriate Attire Policy." *Journal of Homosexuality*, *66*(7), 867–895.

Njoku, N., Butler, M., & Beatty, C. C. (2017). Reimagining the historically Black college and university (HBCU) environment: Exposing race secrets and the binding chains of respectability and othermothering. *International Journal of Qualitative Studies in Education*, *30*(8), 783–799.

Opara, I., Lardier Jr, D. T., Garcia-Reid, P., & Reid, R. J. (2020). Measuring intrapersonal psychological empowerment and ethnic identity: highlighting strengths of urban Black girls. *Youth & Society*, 0044118X20970226.

Okeke, N. L., McLaurin, T., Gilliam-Phillips, R., Wagner, D. H., Barnwell, V. J., Johnson, Y. M., ... & Mitchell, J. T. (2021). Awareness and acceptability of HIV pre-exposure prophylaxis (PrEP) among students at two historically Black universities (HBCU): A cross-sectional survey. *BMC Public health*, *21*(1), 1–9.

Perkins, E. L., Chacon, F., Obizoba, C., Stennis, K. B., Wutoh, R., Madison, L., Wells, G., & Turner, D. (2020). Determinants of risky sexual behaviors in an HBCU community. *Journal of Mental Health and Social Behaviour*, *2*(1), 116. 10.33790/jmhsb1100116

Rubinsky, V., & Cooke-Johnson, A. (2017). "Tell me something other than to use a condom and sex is scary": Memorable messages whom and gender minorities wish for and recall about sexual health. *Women's Studies in Communication*, *40*(4), 379–400.

Index

Page numbers followed by t indicate table

For Product Safety Concerns and Information please contact our EU
representative GPSR@taylorandfrancis.com
Taylor & Francis Verlag GmbH, Kaufingerstraße 24, 80331 München, Germany